DIVO

IN THE

SHERIFF COURT

DIVORCE

IN THE

SHERIFF COURT

Fourth Edition

by

S.A. BENNETT, LL.B., Advocate

W. GREEN / Sweet & Maxwell
EDINBURGH
1994

First published 1984
Reprinted 1984
Second edition 1987
Third edition 1991
Fourth edition 1994

© 1994
W. GREEN & SON LTD.

ISBN 0 414 01091 4

A catalogue record for
this book is available
from the British Library

Printed in Great Britain by M. & A. Thomson Litho Ltd., Scotland.

Foreword

by

Sheriff Principal R. C. Hay, C.B.E., W.S.

It is ten years since the first edition of Mr Bennett's *Short Guide to Divorce in the Sheriff Court* was published. Its publication coincided with the introduction of divorce jurisdiction in the sheriff court, and it provided then, as now, a clear, concise and helpful guide for the practitioner.

Since then the work has gone through successive editions, each reflecting the development of the law both by statute and by judicial decisions. As edition succeeds edition, the book becomes ever more useful as a work of reference for all who deal with divorce in the sheriff court.

The publication of the fourth edition is again timely. Mr Bennett has substantially rewritten Chapter 1 and has revised the other chapters so as to provide a clear but always concise guide to the provisions of the new Ordinary Cause Rules in relation to family actions which came into force on January 1, 1994. He has also comprehensively updated the references to recent judicial decisions, particularly in the important and often difficult area of financial provision on divorce.

I have pleasure in commending the latest edition of this invaluable and now standard work to all in the profession who are involved with divorce in the sheriff court. There will be few practitioners in this field who can afford to be without it.

Paisley
May 24, 1994 R. C. Hay

PREFACE

I wish to thank Craig Paterson for preparing the index, Selina Rae for typing the script and David Nicol of Messrs Allan McDougal & Co., S.S.C. for expertly reviewing the text.

Edinburgh,   SIGGI BENNETT.
May 1994

CONTENTS

Contents

Table of Cases

Table of Cases xiii

Table of Statutes

Table of Ordinary Cause Rules

CHAPTER 1

PROCEDURE PECULIAR TO DIVORCE[1]

THE ordinary cause rules include special provisions applicable to actions of divorce. Some of these rules are drawn to the attention of practitioners under the relevant subject heading (*e.g.* mental disorder). Others are mentioned in this chapter.

CITATION AND INTIMATION

Citation
Except where the address of the defender is not known to the pursuer and cannot reasonably be ascertained, citation of the defender requires to be in Form F15, which must be attached to a copy of the initial writ and warrant of citation in Form F14 and must have appended to it a notice of intention to defend in Form F26[2] The certificate of citation requires to be in Form F16 which must be attached to the initial writ.[3]

Where the address of the defender is not known to the pursuer and cannot reasonably be ascertained, citation of the defender is effected in accordance with rule 5.6,[4] which provides as follows:

"(1) Where the address of a person to be cited or served with a document is not known and cannot reasonably be ascertained, the sheriff shall grant warrant for citation or service upon that person—
(a) by the publication of an advertisement in Form G3 in a specified newspaper circulating in the area of the last known address of that person, or

---

[1] For the purposes of this Chapter, "divorce" is taken to include other family actions (as defined in r. 33.1 (1)), as appropriate.

[2] rr. 33.10 and 33.11 (1). As to service in cases of mental disorder of defender, see r. 33.13 (set forth in Chap. 2, n. 50).

[3] r. 33.11 (2).

[4] r. 5.6 applies to all ordinary causes. In actions of divorce and other family actions, there is the additional requirement of intimation in terms of r. 33.7 (1)(*a*) and (6) (as to which, see text accompanying nn. 10 and 26 *infra*). The pursuer must also aver in the condescendence what steps have been taken to ascertain the defender's present whereabouts—r. 3.1(6).

(b)   by displaying on the walls of court a copy of the instance and crave of the initial writ, the warrant of citation and a notice in Form G4;

and the period of notice fixed by the sheriff shall run from the date of publication of the advertisement or display on the walls of court, as the case may be.

(2) Where service requires to be executed under paragraph (1), the pursuer shall lodge a service copy of the initial writ and a copy of any warrant of citation with the sheriff clerk from whom they may be uplifted by the person for whom they are intended.

(3) Where a person has been cited or served in accordance with paragraph (1) and, after the cause has commenced, his address becomes known, the sheriff may allow the initial writ to be amended subject to such conditions as to re-service, intimation, expenses or transfer of the cause as he thinks fit.

(4) Where advertisement in a newspaper is required for the purpose of citation or service under this rule, a copy of the newspaper containing the advertisement shall be lodged with the sheriff clerk by the pursuer.

(5) Where display on the walls of court is required under paragraph (1)(b), the pursuer shall supply to the sheriff clerk for that purpose a certified copy of the instance and crave of the initial writ and any warrant of citation.''

Intimation

The sheriff may order intimation of an action[5] to be made to such person as he thinks fit.[6] A crave[7] or motion[8] to dispense with intimation may be granted by him.

Rule 33.7 (1) requires the pursuer to include in the initial writ[9] a crave for a warrant for intimation—

---

[5] Intimation of motions and other matters falls to be made in terms of, *e.g.*, rr. 33.25, 33.40, 33.42, 33.69 (2) and 33.70 (2). Where no notice of intention to defend has been lodged, motions do not require to be intimated—rr. 15.2 and 33.33.

[6] r. 33.15 (1). Whenever he considers it necessary for the proper disposal of an action of divorce, the sheriff must direct that the action be brought to the notice of the Lord Advocate in order that he may determine whether he should enter appearance therein—Sheriff Courts (Scotland) Act 1907, s. 38 B (1). (No expenses are claimable by or against the Lord Advocate in any action in which he has entered appearance under that section (*ibid.*, s. 38 B (2))).

[7] r. 33.7 (5), applicable to pursuers (see text accompanying n. 24 *infra*).

[8] rr. 33.7 (6) and 33.15 (2), applicable to any party (see text accompanying nn. 26 and 23 *infra*).

[9] In the event that the pursuer makes an application or averment which, had it been made in the initial writ, would have required a warrant for intimation under r. 33.7, she requires to lodge a motion for warrant for intimation or to dispense with such intimation—r. 33.15 (2).

(a) in an action where the address of the defender is not known to the pursuer and cannot reasonably be ascertained, to—

    (i) every child of the marriage between the parties who has reached the age of 16 years, and

    (ii) one of the next-of-kin of the defender who has reached that age,

unless the address of such a person is not known to the pursuer and cannot reasonably be ascertained, and a notice of intimation in Form F1 shall be attached to the copy of the initial writ intimated to any such person[10];

(b) in an action where the pursuer alleges that the defender has committed adultery[11] with another person, to that person, unless—

    (i) that person is not named in the initial writ and, if the adultery is relied on for the purposes of section 1 (2)(*a*) of the Divorce (Scotland) Act 1976 (irretrievable breakdown of marriage by reason of adultery), the initial writ contains an averment that his or her identity is not known to the pursuer and cannot reasonably be ascertained, or

    (ii) the pursuer alleges that the defender has been guilty of rape upon or incest with that named person,

and a notice of intimation in Form F2 shall be attached to the copy of the initial writ intimated to any such person[12];

(c) in an action where the defender is a person who is suffering from a mental disorder, to—

    (i) those persons mentioned in sub-paragraph (a)(i) and (ii), *supra*, unless the address of such person is not known to the pursuer and cannot reasonably be ascertained, and

    (ii) the *curator bonis* to the defender, if one has been appointed,

and a notice of intimation in Form F3 shall be attached to the copy of the initial writ intimated to any such person[13];

---

[10] r. 33.7 (1)(*a*).

[11] In the event that the pursuer alleges an "improper association" (namely sodomy, incest or any homosexual relationship) between the defender and another named person, r. 33.8 applies (Chap. 3, n. 33).

[12] r. 33.7 (1)(*b*).

[13] r. 33.7 (1)(*c*).

(d) in an action relating to a marriage which was entered into under a law which permits polygamy where—
    (i)   one of the decrees specified in section 2(2) of the Matrimonial Proceedings (Polygamous Marriages) Act 1972 is sought, and
    (ii) either party to the marriage in question has any spouse additional to the other party,
to any such additional spouse, and a notice of intimation in Form F4 shall be attached to the initial writ intimated to any such person[14];

(e) in an action where the sheriff may make an order for any parental rights in respect of a child—
    (i)   who is in the care of a local authority, to that authority and a notice of intimation in Form F5 shall be attached to the initial writ intimated to that authority;
    (ii) who, being a child of one party to the marriage, has been accepted as a child of the family by the other party to the marriage and who is liable to be maintained by a third party, to that third party, and a notice of intimation in Form F5 shall be attached to the initial writ intimated to that third party; or
    (iii) in respect of whom a third party exercises such rights *de facto*, to that third party, and a notice of intimation in Form F6 shall be attached to the initial writ intimated to that third party[15];

(f) in an action where the pursuer craves the custody of a child, to any parent or guardian of the child who is not a party to the action, and a notice of intimation in Form F7 shall be attached to the initial writ intimated to any such parent or guardian[16];

(g) in an action where the pursuer craves the custody of a child and the pursuer is—
    (i)   not a parent of that child, and
    (ii) resident in Scotland when the initial writ is lodged,
to the local authority within which area the pursuer resides, and a notice of intimation in Form F8 shall be attached to the initial writ intimated to that authority[17];

---

[14] r. 33.7 (1)(*d*).
[15] r. 33.7 (1)(*e*).
[16] r. 33.7 (1)(*f*).
[17] r. 33.7 (1)(*g*). Rule 33.7(4) requires a pursuer not resident in Scotland who craves custody of a child to include a crave for an order for intimation in Form F8 to

(h) in an action which affects a child, to that child if not a party to the action, and a notice of intimation in Form F9 shall be attached to the initial writ intimated to that child[18];

(i) in an action where the pursuer makes an application for an order under section 8(1)(*aa*) of the Family Law (Scotland) Act 1985 (transfer of property) and—

    (i) the consent of a third party to such a transfer is necessary by virtue of an obligation, enactment or rule of law, or

    (ii) the property is subject to a security,

to the third party or creditor, as the case may be, and a notice of intimation in Form F10 shall be attached to the initial writ intimated to any such person[19];

(j) in an action where the pursuer makes an application for an order under section 18 of the 1985 Act (which relates to avoidance transactions), to—

---

such local authority as the sheriff thinks fit. (Note that this provision, like r. 33.7 (1)(*g*), is designed to give effect to s. 49 of the Children Act 1975; since, in terms of subs. (1), s. 49 only applies where the applicant for custody of a child is not a parent of the child, r. 33.7(4) should presumably be construed accordingly).

[18] r. 33.7 (1)(*h*). This rule has been introduced to comply with Article 12 of the UN Convention on the Rights of the Child 1989 (Commentary on New Ordinary Cause Rules, Sheriff Court Rules Council, p. 14), which is in the following terms:

"1. States Parties shall assure to the child who is capable of forming his or her own views the right to express those views freely in all matters affecting the child, the views of the child being given due weight in accordance with the age and maturity of the child.

2. For this purpose, the child shall in particular be provided the opportunity to be heard in any judicial and administrative proceedings affecting the child, either directly, or through a representative or an appropriate body, in a manner consistent with the procedural rules of national law."

The phrase "child who is capable of forming his or her own views" would seem generally to include a child of 12 years or more (*cf.* Age of Legal Capacity (Scotland) Act 1991, s. 2 (2) and (3) and Family Law (Scotland) Bill, cll. 6 (2) and 12 (5) (App.VII)) and might include a child of eight years or more (*cf.* Scottish Law Commission, *Report on Family Law*, (Scot. Law Com. No. 135, 1992), para. 5.25, and Criminal Procedure (Scotland) Act 1975, s. 170) and possibly one of even lesser years (*Russell* v. *Russell*, 1991 S.C.L.R. 429 (girl of 6)). For a discussion of circumstances in which intimation is or is not important, see (1994) 39 J.L.S. 55, 56. See also (1994) 39 J.L.S.7. An action of divorce involving a parent or parents affects a child whether or not an order for parental rights is craved, it is thought (*cf.* Matrimonial Proceedings (Children) Act 1958, s. 8(1).

[19] r. 13.7 (1)(*i*).

      (i)   any third party in whose favour the transfer of, or transaction involving, the property is to be or was made, and

     (ii) any other person having an interest in the transfer of, or transaction involving, the property,

and a notice of intimation in Form F11 shall be attached to the initial writ intimated to any such person[20]; and

  (k) in an action where the pursuer makes an application for an order under the Matrimonial Homes (Family Protection) (Scotland) Act 1981, where the application is under section 3(1), 3(2), 4, 7, 13 or 18 of that Act, and the entitled spouse is a tenant or occupies the matrimonial home by permission of a third party, to the landlord or the third party, as the case may be, and a notice of intimation in Form F12 shall be attached to the initial writ intimated to any such person.[21]

Each notice of intimation must be on a period of notice of 21 days unless the sheriff otherwise orders; but the sheriff cannot order a period of notice of less than two days.[22]

Where a party makes an application or averment which, had it been made in an initial writ, would have required a warrant for intimation under rule 33.7, that party must lodge a motion for warrant for intimation or to dispense with such intimation.[23]

Where the address of a person mentioned in paragraphs (b), (d), (e), (f), (h), (i), (j) or (k) *supra* is not known and cannot reasonably be ascertained, there must be a crave in the initial writ to dispense with intimation (otherwise a motion to that effect); and the sheriff may grant that crave (otherwise motion) or make such other order as he thinks fit.[24]

Where the identity or address of any person in respect of whom a warrant for intimation requires to be applied for is not known and cannot reasonably be ascertained, the party required to apply for the warrant must include in his pleadings an averment of that fact and averments setting out what steps have been taken to ascertain the identity or address, as the case may be, of that person.[25]

---

[20] r. 13.7 (1)(*j*).
[21] r. 13.7 (1)(*k*).
[22] r. 33.7 (3).
[23] r. 33.15 (2).
[24] r. 33.7 (5) and text accompanying preceding footnote.
[25] r. 33.4.

Where the identity or address of a person to whom intimation is required becomes known during the course of the action, the party who would have been required to insert a warrant for intimation to that person must lodge a motion for a warrant for intimation to that person or to dispense with such intimation.[26]

PROOF

The requirement of proof

In an action of divorce (whether or not appearance has been entered for the defender), no decree or judgment in favour of the pursuer shall be pronounced until the grounds of action have been established by evidence.[27]

As a consequence of this requirement of proof, default by the defender in an action of divorce entitles the sheriff only to allow the case to proceed as undefended.[28]

Affidavits

In actions to which rule 33.28 applies, evidence requires to be given by affidavit,[29] unless the sheriff otherwise directs.[30] The rule applies to: (a) actions in which no notice of intention to defend has been lodged; (b) an action in which a curator *ad litem* has been appointed under rule 33.16 where the curator *ad litem* to the defender has lodged a minute intimating that he does not intend to lodge defences; (c) any action which proceeds at any stage as undefended where the sheriff so directs; and (d) the merits of an action which is undefended on the merits where the sheriff so directs, notwithstanding that the action is defended on an ancillary matter.[31] Where the rule applies, unless the sheriff

---

[26] r. 33.7 (6).

[27] Civil Evidence (Scotland) Act 1988, s. 8(1).

[28] r. 33.37 (2)(*a*).

[29] The applicable Practice Note or Act of Court relative to divorce affidavits should be consulted before affidavit evidence is presented to the court (see App.III). An affidavit sworn prior to the raising of the action is admissible only insofar as it relates to events which occurred before the action was raised (*McInnes* v. *McInnes*, 1990 S.C.L.R. 327). Rule 33.28(4) provides that evidence in the form of a written statement bearing to be the professional opinion of a duly qualified medical practitioner, which has been signed by him and lodged in process, shall be admissible in place of parole evidence by him.

[30] r. 33.28(2). Note that at any proof in an undefended action, it is not necessary to record the evidence—r. 33.32.

[31] r. 33.28(1).

otherwise directs, evidence relating to the welfare of a child must be given by affidavit, at least one affidavit being emitted by a person other than a parent or party to the action.[32]

In an action to which rule 33.28 applies, the pursuer must at any time after the expiry of the period for lodging a notice of intention to defend: (a) lodge in process the affidavit evidence; and (b) endorse a minute in Form F27 on the initial writ.[33]

A minute in Form F27 is as follows:

> "(*Insert name of solicitor for the pursuer*) having considered the evidence contained in the affidavits and the other documents all as specified in the Schedule hereto and being satisfied that upon the evidence a motion for decree (in terms of the crave(s)[34] of the initial writ) [*or in such restricted terms as may be appropriate*][35] may properly be made, moves the court accordingly.
>
> > In respect whereof
> > Signed
> > Solicitor for the pursuer (*add designation and business address*)
>
> > > SCHEDULE
> > (*Number and specify documents*[36] *considered*)."

The sheriff may at any time after the pursuer has complied with the foregoing,[37] without requiring the appearance of parties, grant

---

[32] r. 33.28(3).

[33] r. 33.29(1).

[34] Note that r. 33.26 entitles the sheriff to grant decree in respect of those parts of a joint minute in relation to which he could otherwise make an order, whether or not such a decree would include a matter for which there was no crave.

[35] Illustrations of "restricted terms" are as follows:

    (i)   ... for decree in terms of the first, third and fourth craves of the initial writ ...

    (ii)   ... for decree in terms of the first crave and the joint minute no. 10 of process ...

    (iii) ... for decree in terms of the first and second craves, and, in relation to the third crave (for a periodical allowance) for the sum craved or for such other sum as the court thinks fit ...

[36] Such documents include affidavits, the parties' marriage certificate and the birth certificate of any child of the marriage or accepted into the family as well as any notice of consent or joint minute and any extract decree or conviction, photograph, medical report or other production relevant to the case. Each witness should docquet any production relative to his or her evidence and refer to that production by its process number in his or her affidavit. The pursuer should identify the defender's signature on any document signed by him (*e.g.* joint minute, notice of consent).

[37] Subject to the rule of law that an action falls if no procedure has followed within a year and a day of the expiry of the period of notice—*McCulloch* v. *McCulloch*,

decree in terms of the motion for decree; or may remit the cause for such further procedure, including proof by parole evidence, as he thinks fit.[38]

The sheriff may accept evidence by affidavit at any hearing for an order or interim order.[39]

DEFENDED ACTIONS

Part III of Chapter 33 of the ordinary cause rules comprises rules applicable to actions of divorce which are defended.

Rule 33.34 makes provision regarding notices of intention to defend and defences, applying[40] where the defender seeks—

(a) to oppose any crave in the initial writ;

(b) to make a claim for—

    (i) aliment[41];

    (ii) an order for financial provision[42]; or

    (iii) an order relating to parental rights[43];

(c) an order—

    (i) under section 16 (1)(b) or (3) of the Family Law (Scotland) Act 1985 (setting aside or varying agreement as to financial provision)[44];

    (ii) under section 18 of the 1985 Act (which relates to avoidance provisions)[45]; or

    (iii) under the Matrimonial Homes (Family Protection) (Scotland) Act 1981; or

(d) to challenge the jurisdiction of the court.

In such an action, the defender must—

(a) lodge a notice of intention to defend in Form F26 before the expiry of the period of notice; and

1990 S.L.T. (Sh.Ct.) 63 and *Dunnett* v. *Dunnett*, 1990 S.C.L.R. 135 (*cf. Donnelly* v. *Donnelly*, 1991 S.L.T. (Sh.Ct.) 9 (rule of law inapplicable where action defended for a time)).

[38] r. 33.29(2).
[39] r. 33.27.
[40] r. 33.34 (1).
[41] Also provided for by r. 33.39 (1)(*a*) and (2)(*b*).
[42] Also provided for by r. 33.48 (1)(*a*) and (2)(*a*).
[43] Also provided for by r. 33.39 (1)(*a*) and (2)(*a*).
[44] Also provided for by r. 33.48 (1)(*a*) and (2)(*b*).
[45] Also provided for by r. 33.48 (1)(*a*) and (2)(*c*).

(b)   make any claim or seek any order, as above referred to, in
those defences by setting out in his defences—
   (i)   craves;
   (ii) averments in the answers to the condescendence in
         support of those craves; and
   (iii) appropriate pleas-in-law.[46]

Notwithstanding abandonment by a pursuer, the court may
allow a defender to pursue an order or claim sought in his
defences; and the proceedings in relation to that order or claim
shall continue in dependence as if a separate cause.[47]

Rule 33.36 requires all parties, except on cause shown, to attend
personally the Options Hearing.[48]

Provision is made by rule 33.37 for the granting of decree by
default, the rule applying[49] in an action in which the defender has
lodged a notice of intention to defend where a party fails—

---

[46] r. 33.34 (2).

[47] r. 33.35.

[48] The Options Hearing is a hearing under r. 9.12. In terms of para. (1) thereof, the
sheriff must at the hearing seek to secure the expeditious progress of the cause
by ascertaining from the parties the matters in dispute and information about
any other matter referred to in para. (3), it being the parties' duty in terms of
para. (2) to provide the sheriff with sufficient information to enable him to
conduct the hearing as provided for in the rule. Paragraph (3) requires the
sheriff, except where the cause is ordered to proceed under additional
procedure, to close the record and (a) appoint the cause to a proof and make
such orders as to the extent of proof, the lodging of a joint minute of admissions
or agreement, or such other matter as he thinks fit; (b) after having heard parties
and considered any note of basis of preliminary plea, appoint the cause to a
proof before answer and make such orders as to the extent of proof, the lodging
of a joint minute of admissions or agreement, or such other matter as he thinks
fit; or (c) after having heard parties and considered any note of basis of
preliminary plea, appoint the cause to a debate if satisfied that there is a
preliminary matter of law which justifies a debate. Paragraph (4) empowers the
sheriff, having heard parties (a) of his own motion or on the motion of any party,
and (b) on being satisfied that the difficulty or complexity of the cause makes it
unsuitable for the standard procedure, to order that the cause proceed under the
additional procedure. Paragraph (5) enables the sheriff, on cause shown, of his
motion or on the motion of any party, to allow a continuation of the Options
Hearing on one occasion only for a period not exceeding 28 days or to the first
suitable court day thereafter. Paragraph (6) provides that on closing the record:
(a) where there are no adjustments made since the lodging of the record under r.
9.11 (2), that record shall become the closed record; and (b) where there are such
adjustments, the sheriff may order that a closed record including such
adjustments be lodged within 7 days after the date of the interlocutor closing the
record.

[49] r. 33.37 (1).

(a) to lodge, or intimate the lodging of, any production or part of process,

(b) to implement an order of the sheriff within a specified period, or

(c) to appear or be represented at any diet.

Where a party has so failed, and is thereby in default, the sheriff may—

(i) allow the action to proceed as undefended under Part II of Chapter 33 of the rules; or

(ii) grant decree of absolvitor; or

(iii) dismiss the action or any claim made or order sought; and

(iv) award expenses.[50]

Where no party appears at a diet, the sheriff may dismiss the action.[51]

The sheriff may, on cause shown, prorogate the time for lodging any production or part of process, or for intimating or implementing any order.[52]

SIMPLIFIED PROCEDURE

Simplified divorce applications (*viz.* applications for divorce by a party to a marriage made in the manner prescribed by rule 33.74) may be made if, but only if—

(a) the applicant relies on the facts set out in section 1(2)(*d*) (no cohabitation for two years with consent of defender to decree), or section 1(2)(*e*) (no cohabitation for five years) of the Divorce (Scotland) Act 1976;

(b) in an application under section 1(2)(*d*) of the 1976 Act, the other party consents to decree of divorce being granted;

(c) no other proceedings are pending in any court which could have the effect of bringing the marriage to an end;

(d) there are no children of the marriage under the age of 16 years;

(e) neither party to the marriage applies for an order for financial provision on divorce; and

---

[50] r. 33.37 (2).
[51] r. 33.37 (3).
[52] r. 33.37 (4).

(f)   neither party to the marriage suffers from mental disorder.[53]

If an application ceases to be one to which the foregoing applies at any time before final decree, it shall be deemed to be abandoned and shall be dismissed.[54]

Rule 33.74 provides that:

> "(1) A simplified divorce application in which the facts set out in section 1(2)(d) ... are relied on shall be made in Form F31 and shall only be of effect if—(a) it is signed by the applicant[55]; and (b) the form of consent in Part 2 of Form F32 is signed by the party to the marriage giving consent.
>
> (2) A simplified divorce application in which the facts set out in section 1(2)(e) ... are relied on shall be made in Form F33 and shall only be of effect if it is signed by the applicant."

It is the duty of the sheriff clerk to cite any person and intimate any document in connection with a simplified divorce application[56] and such requires to be done in accordance with rules 33.76 and 33.77.

Any person on whom service or intimation of a simplified divorce application has been made may give notice by letter sent to the sheriff clerk that he challenges the jurisdiction of the court[57] or opposes the grant of decree of divorce and giving the reasons for his opposition to the application[58]; and in that event, the sheriff must dismiss the application unless he is satisfied that the reasons given for the opposition are frivolous.[59]

Parole evidence cannot be given in a simplified divorce application.[60]

Any appeal against an interlocutor granting decree of divorce in terms of the simplified divorce application may be made,

---

[53] r. 33.73(1) and (3).

[54] r. 33.73(2).

[55] The applicant requires also to send an extract or certified copy of the marriage certificate and the appropriate fee—r. 33.75.

[56] r. 33.76(2).

[57] The sending of such a letter does not imply acceptance of the jurisdiction of the court—r. 33.78(4).

[58] r. 33.78(1).

[59] r. 33.78(2). As to "frivolous", see *Waugh* v. *Waugh*, 1992 S.L.T. (Sh.Ct.) 17. An application was dismissed where a question arose as to the validity of the marriage in *Aranda* v. *Aranda*, 1990 S.L.T. (Sh.Ct.) 101.

[60] r. 33.79.

within 14 days after the date of decree, by sending a letter to the court giving reasons for the appeal.[61]

Any application to the court after decree of divorce has been granted in a simplified divorce application which could have been made if it had been made in an action of divorce shall be made by minute.[62]

---

[61] r. 33.81. As to "reasons for the appeal," see *Colville* v. *Colville*, 1988 S.L.T. (Sh.Ct.) 23 and *Norris* v. *Norris*, 1992 S.L.T. (Sh.Ct.) 51.

[62] r. 33.82. See Chap. 7, n. 18.

CHAPTER 2

MISCELLANEOUS TOPICS

RECONCILIATION[1]

ONE of the aims of the Divorce (Scotland) Act 1976, according to its long title, is "to facilitate reconciliation of the parties in consistorial causes."

Section 2 of the Act contains certain provisions for the encouragement of reconciliation between spouses.[2] The court is empowered by that provision in appropriate cases to continue any pending action of divorce for such period as it thinks proper to enable attempts to be made to effect reconciliation (and any cohabitation during this period is disregarded for the purposes of that action).[3] Practitioners have been enjoined by a Court of Session Practice Note[4] to:

> "try to identify, at as early a stage as possible, those cases in which the parties might benefit from the expert advice and guidance of a marriage counsellor, and in those cases [to] encourage the parties to seek such advice and guidance."

PROOF OF MARRIAGE

As a prerequisite to obtaining decree of divorce, the pursuer must aver and prove the parties' marriage. It is sufficient for the pursuer to give evidence of the date and place of the marriage

---

[1] Not to be confused with conciliation, as to which see Chap. 6, text accompanying n. 33.
[2] Those provisions affecting the merits of divorce actions are noticed in Chap. 3, text accompanying nn. 28, 39 and 44.
[3] s.2(1).
[4] March 11, 1977.

ceremony.[5] However, unless the sheriff otherwise directs, a warrant for citation will not be granted without there being produced with the initial writ an extract[6] of the relevant entry in the register of marriages or an equivalent document.[7] Such a direction, it is thought, would be justified where a warrant is required as a matter of urgency (and an undertaking to lodge the certificate within a certain period of time is given) or where it is impossible to obtain relevant documentation and it is intended to prove the marriage by parole evidence.

JURISDICTION

A sheriff court has jurisdiction by virtue of section 8(2) of the Domicile and Matrimonial Proceedings Act 1973[8] to entertain an action for divorce if (and only if[9])

(a)   either party to the marriage in question—

     (i)   is *domiciled* in Scotland at the date when the action is begun,[10] or

    (ii)   was *habitually resident* there throughout the period of one year ending with that date;

and

(b)   either party to the marriage—

---

[5] Civil Evidence (Scotland) Act 1988, s.1(1). If the marriage is disputed, certain statutory provisions may fall to be applied (as to which, see Clive, pp. 448–451).

[6] Where the defender's whereabouts are unknown, a recently-extracted certificate should be produced (see 1950 S.L.T. (News) 11) unless the parties were married in Scotland, in which event a letter from General Register Office stating that the parties are not already divorced should be lodged (see 1984 S.L.T. (News) 100).

[7] r. 33.9(a). The same applies, where appropriate, in respect of birth certificates—r. 33.9(b).

[8] As amended by the Divorce Jurisdiction, Court Fees and Legal Aid (Scotland) Act 1983, Sched. 1, para. 18.

[9] Prorogation, for example, is not a ground of jurisdiction in actions of divorce— *Singh* v. *Singh*, 1988 S.C.L.R. 541.

[10] *Cf. City of Edinburgh District Council* v. *Davis*, 1987 S.L.T. (Sh.Ct.) 33 (action "raised" when citation of defender effected).

   (i)   was resident in the sheriffdom[11] for a period of 40 days ending with that date,[12] or

  (ii)   was resident in the sheriffdom for a period of not less than 40 days ending not more than 40 days before the said date and has no known residence in Scotland at that date.[13]

A sheriff court also has jurisdiction to entertain an action of divorce begun at a time when a similar action is pending in relation to the marriage in respect of which the court has jurisdiction.[14] Thus if for example a divorce action is raised on the basis of the pursuer's domicile in Scotland and residence within the sheriffdom for the appropriate period and the pursuer then leaves the country for good, the sheriff court in which the divorce action was raised has jurisdiction to entertain a further action of divorce for as long as the original action is pending. The foregoing provisions are without prejudice to any sheriff court's jurisdiction to entertain an action of divorce remitted to it in pursuance of any enactment or rule of court.[15]

There remains to be considered the meaning of the terms "domicile" and "habitual residence."

Domicile

As the following quotation[16] indicates, "domicile"[17] is a term not readily defined:

> "the concept of domicile is a complicated one, and it is possible

---

[11] There seems to be nothing as a matter of law to require the raising of the action in the *sheriff court district* in which the party was resident. As a matter of practice, however, special cause must be shown to obtain warrant for citation from any court within a sheriffdom other than that in which the cause would normally fall to be dealt, *viz.* the court within the district of which the relevant party was resident (see *Simpson* v. *Bruce*, 1984 S.L.T. (Sh.Ct.) 38).

[12] Residence within the sheriffdom thereafter cannot be taken into account in determining whether or not there is jurisdiction—*McNeill* v. *McNeill*, 1960 S.C. 30.

[13] There would appear to be no room to interpret s.8(2)(*b*)(ii) in anything other than a literal fashion: *cf. McNeill; Fraser* v. *Macfadyen* (1940) 56 Sh.Ct.Rep. 66; and *Hutchinson* v. *Goodale*, 1940 S.L.T. (Sh.Ct.) 24.

[14] 1973 Act, s.8(3).

[15] 1973 Act, s.8(4). An example of an action of divorce remitted to the sheriff court is *Gribb* v. *Gribb*, 1992 S.C.L.R. 776.

[16] Anton, *Private International Law* (2nd ed. 1990), p. 125.

[17] "Domicile" is separately defined for the purposes of the Civil Jurisdiction and Judgments Act 1982 by ss.44–46 of that Act. By virtue of Sched. 9, para. 1 thereof, the 1982 Act does not govern jurisdiction in actions of divorce.

merely to state the circumstances in which Scots law will impute to a person a domicile within a particular country. In epitome, Scots law imputes to a legitimate child at his birth the domicile of his father and to an illegitimate or posthumous child [the father having died] the domicile of his mother. This is his domicile of origin. . . . [Until he attains the age of 16 years] his domicile changes with that of the person upon whom he is dependent.[18] . . . [Thereafter][19] his existing domicile continues to be attributed to him unless and until he resides in a different country, with the intention of residing there permanently. If these elements of fact and intention concur, he is then attributed a domicile in that country, called a domicile of choice. Scots law will continue to infer that he is domiciled in the country of choice either until he leaves that country with the settled intention of abandoning it as a home, when he is deemed to revert to

---

[18] By virtue of s.4 of the 1973 Act, when his parents are alive but living apart, a child's dependent domicile shall be that of his mother if (a) he then has his home with her and has no home with his father; or (b) he has at any time had her domicile by virtue of para. (*a*) and has not since had a home with his father; and if his mother then dies and he has not since had a home with his father the child has the domicile which she last had before she died. The Scottish Law Commission in their *Report on Family Law* (Scot. Law Com. No. 135, 1992) propose the following enactment relative to the domicile of children:

"45.—(1) A child is domiciled in the country with which he or she is for the time being most closely connected.

(2) Where the child's parents are domiciled in the same country and the child has his or her home with either or both of them, it is to be presumed, unless the contrary is shown, that the child is most closely connected with that country.

(3) Where the child's parents are not domiciled in the same country and the child has his or her home with one of them, but not with the other, it is to be presumed, unless the contrary is shown, that the child is most closely connected with the country in which the parent with whom the child has his or her home is domiciled.

(4) The rule laid down by the foregoing provisions of this section apply to times before this Act comes into force but only for the purpose of determining where at any time after this Act comes into force a child is domiciled.

(5) Where those rules apply, they do so in place of the corresponding rules of the common law and section 4 of the Domicile and Matrimonial Proceedings Act 1973 and section 9(1)(*a*) of the Law Reform (Parent and Child) (Scotland) Act 1986.

(6) In this section—

'child' means a person who has not attained the age of 16 years;

'country' includes territory and means, in relation to a person whose domicile at a particular time is in question, a country which has its own system of law at that time."

[19] By virtue of s.7 of the Age of Legal Capacity (Scotland) Act 1991, the time at which a person first becomes capable of having an independent domicile is the date at which he attains the age of 16 years.

his domicile of origin, or until he acquires a domicile of choice in another country."

Facts from which domicile may be inferred should be averred.[20]

Habitual residence

The term "habitual residence" was considered in *Morris* v. *Morris*,[21] wherein the sheriff principal observed: "Habitual residence has not been defined. At the end of the day it is a question of fact. Without seeking to lay down any definition I would consider that it encompasses the idea of where the person normally lives." In the Scottish Law Commission's report[22] on which the 1973 Act was based there is averred a justification for use of that particular term:

> "... to indicate that it is not enough for a person to make his occasional residence within the territory but that, on the other hand, residence which in substance is stable should not be ignored because the person in question occasionally interrupts it to go elsewhere for purposes of business or recreation."

CONCURRENT PROCEEDINGS[23]

Where more than one legal system has jurisdiction to divorce the parties to a marriage, complex rules are required to avoid conflicts of jurisdiction.

These rules are to be found in Schedule 3 to the Domicile and Matrimonial Proceedings Act 1973. Broadly speaking, they require the parties to certain Scottish actions (including actions of divorce) to tell the court about any proceedings continuing outwith Scotland which are in respect of the marriage or capable of affecting its validity or subsistence (hereinafter referred to as "concurrent proceedings"); and they make provision (discussed *infra*) regarding mandatory and discretionary sists by the Scottish court where there are concurrent proceedings elsewhere.

---

[20] *Horn* v. *Horn*, 1935 S.L.T. 589. See also *Spence* v. *Spence*, unreported, Outer House, March 9, 1994 (Lord Cullen).

[21] 1993 S.C.L.R. 144 at p. 145. See also *Cruse* v. *Chittum*, [1947] 2 All E.R. 940, *Hack* v. *Hack* (1976) 6 Fam.Law 177, *Oundjian* v. *Oundjian* [1980] F.L.R. 198 and *Kapur* v. *Kapur* [1984] F.L.R. 920.

[22] *Report on Jurisdiction in Consistorial Cases affecting Matrimonial Status* (Scot. Law Com. No. 25, 1972), at para. 71.

[23] See Chap. 6, text accompanying nn. 38 and 39, regarding concurrent proceedings concerning children.

This duty on parties to inform the court of any concurrent proceedings subsists while the action is pending and until proof in the action has begun.[24] Failure of a person to perform this duty prolongs the time within which the court has a discretion to sist the cause (which discretion would otherwise cease to be exercisable at the beginning of the proof).[25]

Ordinary cause rule 33.2 provides the machinery whereby each party may discharge this duty.

The pursuer must state in the condescendence of the initial writ whether to her knowledge any proceedings are continuing[26] in Scotland or in any other country which are in respect of the marriage to which the initial writ relates or are capable of affecting its validity or subsistence.[27]

Where such proceedings are continuing, the pursuer must also state:

  (a) the court, tribunal or authority before which they have been commenced;

  (b) the date of commencement;

  (c) the names of the parties;

  (d) the date or expected date of any proof (or its equivalent) in the proceedings; and

  (e) such other facts as may be relevant to the question of whether or not the action before the sheriff should be sisted under Schedule 3 to the 1973 Act (discussed *infra*).[28]

Where such proceedings are continuing; the action before the sheriff is defended; and either (i) the initial writ does not contain the statement anent those proceedings above referred to, or (ii) the particulars mentioned in (a) to (e) above are incomplete or incorrect, any defences or minute, as the case may be, lodged by any person to the action must include that statement and, where appropriate, the further or correct particulars.[29]

Mandatory sists

Where before the beginning of the proof in a continuing divorce

---

[24] Sched. 3, para. 7. Neither the taking of evidence on commission nor a separate proof relating to any preliminary plea is to be regarded as part of the proof in the action: Sched. 3, para. 4(a); *quaere* when proof could be said to begin where evidence is submitted in the form of affidavits.

[25] para. 9(1) and (4); there is no other sanction in respect of such failure: para. 9(4).

[26] Proceedings are "continuing" at any time after they have commenced and before they have been finally disposed of—r. 33.1.(3).

[27] r. 33.2(2)(*a*).

[28] r. 33.2(2)(*b*).

[29] r. 33.2(3).

action it appears to the court, on the application[30] of a party to the marriage, that proceedings in respect of that marriage for divorce or nullity of marriage are continuing in a related jurisdiction (*i.e.* another country within the United Kingdom[31]) and certain other conditions are satisfied, the court *must* sist the action.[32]

These other conditions are that it appears to the court:

(1)   that the parties to the marriage have resided together after the marriage was contracted;

(2)   that the place where they resided together when the action in the Scots court was begun (or, if they did not then reside together, where they last resided together before that date) is in that related jurisdiction; and

(3)   that either party was habitually resident in that related jurisdiction throughout the year ending with the date on which they last resided together before the action in the Scots court was begun.

Thus if A and his spouse reside together after their marriage and at some stage live in, say, England where they reside continuously for over a year before separating; and thereafter they go their separate ways, raising actions of divorce in Scotland and England respectively, the Scottish court must be informed of the proceedings continuing in England and must sist A's action in Scotland. The sist would not be mandatory if the last place where A and his spouse resided together before the Scots action was raised was not England, or if neither A nor his spouse was habitually resident in England for the year prior to their separation.

Where an action has been sisted by reference to proceedings in a related jurisdiction, the Scots court loses the power to make "relevant orders" in that action, namely interim orders in relation to aliment for a spouse or a child, custody or removal of children or for the committing of the care of a child to an individual.[33] Any such order ceases to have effect three months from the date of the sisting of the action (unless the order or the sist has by then been recalled).[34] These provisions are subject to the court's power to make, or extend the duration of, a relevant order if the court

---

[30] Application must be made by written motion—r. 33.17.

[31] Namely, England, Wales, Northern Ireland, Jersey, Guernsey (including Alderney and Sark) and the Isle of Man—para. 3(2).

[32] para. 8.

[33] para. 11(2)(*a*); "relevant orders" is defined in para. 11(1).

[34] para. 11(2)(*b*).

considers such to be necessary "as a matter of necessity and urgency."[35]

If at the time of the sisting of the Scots action there is in force, or if thereafter there comes into force, in the proceedings elsewhere an order in relation to any of four specified matters, that order supersedes any similar order in the Scots action that has been, or might be, made.[36] These four matters are:

(1) periodical payments for a spouse;
(2) periodical payments for a child;
(3) the custody of (or access to) a child; and
(4) the education of a child.

These provisions have no effect on the power of the court to make relevant orders once the sist has been recalled; to vary or recall relevant orders still in force; or to enforce any relevant order as respects any period when it is or was in force.[37]

The court may on the application of a party to the action recall a mandatory sist if it appears to the court that the proceedings elsewhere are sisted or concluded or that the prosecution of them has been unreasonably delayed.[38] Once the sist has been recalled, the rule on mandatory sists has no further application.[39]

Discretionary sists

Where before the beginning of the proof[40] in a continuing divorce action it appears to the court that there are concurrent proceedings in another jurisdiction (*i.e.* outwith the United Kingdom) the court *may* sist the action.[41]

Its discretion to do so is to be exercised if it appears to the court that the balance of fairness (including convenience) as between the parties to the marriage is such that it is appropriate for those other proceedings to be disposed of before further steps are taken in the Scots action.[42] In considering the balance of fairness and convenience, the court requires to have regard to all factors appearing to be relevant, including the convenience of witnesses and any delay or expense which may result from the proceedings

---

[35] para. 11(2)(c).
[36] para. 11(3); including any order judged to be necessary as a matter of necessity and urgency.
[37] para. 11(4).
[38] para. 10(1). As to the mode of application, see n. 30 *supra*.
[39] para. 10(2).
[40] See n. 24 *supra*.
[41] para. 9(1).
[42] *Ibid*.

being sisted, or not being sisted.[43] It has been held that the proper
initial approach to the question of the balance of fairness
(including convenience) is to consider the overall connection of
the marriage with the jurisdictions in question; and if the overall
connection of the marriage is prima facie with Scotland, the court
would only be entitled to grant the sist if it were to take the view
that there were, nevertheless, other circumstances by reason of
which justice required that a sist should be granted.[44]

The court may on the application of a party to the action recall a
discretionary sist if it appears to the court that the proceedings
elsewhere are sisted or concluded or that the prosecution of them
has been unreasonably delayed.[45]

MENTAL DISORDER

It is not uncommon to come across the problem of mental
disorder in matrimonial disputes leading to the raising of an
action of divorce. The effect of the problem is considered in
relation to both pursuing and defending divorce actions.

Mentally disordered pursuer

An insane person cannot competently pursue an action of
divorce.[46] Mental disorder falling short of insanity does not of
itself preclude the raising of an action of divorce; the pursuer
must however have the capacity to give instructions for the
raising and prosecution of the action.[47] A preliminary proof as to
the pursuer's mental condition is competent; the onus on the
defender to establish incapacity is a heavy one.[48]

Mentally disordered defender

In an action where the defender is a person who is suffering

---

[43] para. 9(2).
[44] *Mitchell* v. *Mitchell*, 1993 S.L.T. 123. See also *De Dampierre* v. *De Dampierre* [1988]
A.C. 92.
[45] para. 10(1). As to the mode of application, see n. 30 *supra*.
[46] *Thomson* v. *Thomson* (1887) 14 R. 634.
[47] *Gibson* v. *Gibson*, 1970 S.L.T. (Notes) 60.
[48] *AB* v. *CB*, 1937 S.C. 408.

from a mental disorder,[49] intimation requires to be made in accordance with r. 33.7(1)(*c*); and where the defender is also resident in a hospital or other similar institution, citation requires to be effected in accordance with r. 33.13.[50]

Rule 33.16 applies where it appears to the court that the defender is suffering from a mental disorder. In that event, the sheriff must:

(a) appoint a curator *ad litem* to the defender;
(b) where the facts set out in section 1(2)(d) of the Divorce (Scotland) Act 1976 (no cohabitation for two years with consent of defender to decree) are relied on—
  (i) make an order for intimation of the ground of the action to the Mental Welfare Commission for Scotland; and
  (ii) include in such an order a requirement that the Commission sends to the sheriff clerk a report indicating whether in its opinion the defender is

---

[49] "Mental disorder" is defined by the Mental Health (Scotland) Act 1984 as "mental illness or mental handicap, however caused or manifested" (s. 1(2)). By virtue of s. 1(3), no person is to be treated as suffering from mental disorder by reason only of promiscuity or other immoral conduct, sexual deviancy or dependence on alcohol or drugs.

[50] As to r. 33.7(1)(*c*), see Chap. 1 (text accompanying n. 13). Rule 33.13 requires citation to be executed by registered post or the first class recorded delivery service addressed to the medical officer in charge of that hospital or institution; and there requires to be included with the copy of the initial writ—
  (a) a citation in Form F15;
  (b) any notice required by rule 33.14(1) (see Chap. 3, nn. 45 and 56 and accompanying text).
  (c) a request in Form F17;
  (d) a form of certificate in Form F18 requesting the medical officer to—
    (i) deliver and explain the initial writ, citation and any notice or form of notice of consent required under rule 33 14(1) personally to the defender; or
    (ii) certify that such delivery or explanation would be dangerous to the health or mental condition of the defender; and
  (e) a stamped envelope addressed for return of that certificate to the pursuer or his solicitor, if he has one.
The medical officer must send the certificate in Form F18 duly completed to the pursuer or his solicitor, as the case may be, and that certificate must be attached to the certificate of citation (r. 33.13(2) and (3)).
Where such a certificate bears that the initial writ has not been delivered to the defender, the sheriff may, at any time before decree
  (a) order such further medical inquiry, and
  (b) make such order for further service or intimation as he thinks fit (r. 33.13 (4)).

capable of deciding whether or not to give consent to the granting of decree.[51]

Within seven days after the appointment of a curator *ad litem*, the pursuer must send to him—

(a)   a copy of the initial writ and any defences (including any adjustments and amendments) lodged; and

(b)   a copy of the notice in Form G5 sent to him by the sheriff clerk.[52]

On receipt of a report from the Commission, the sheriff clerk must—

(a)   lodge the report in process; and

(b)   intimate that this has been done to—

    (i)   the pursuer;

    (ii)   the solicitor for the defender, if known; and

    (iii)   the curator *ad litem*.[53]

The curator *ad litem* requires to lodge in process within 14 days after the report of the Commission has been lodged in process or, where no such report is required, within 21 days after the date of his appointment, one of the following:

(a)   a notice of intention to defend;

(b)   defences to the action;

(c)   a minute adopting defences already lodged; or

(d)   a minute stating that the curator *ad litem* does not intend to lodge defences.[54]

Notwithstanding that he has lodged a minute stating that he does not intend to lodge defences, a curator *ad litem* may appear at any stage of the action to protect the interests of the defender.[55]

If, at any time, it appears to the curator *ad litem* that the defender is not suffering from mental disorder, he may report that fact to the court and seek his own discharge.[56]

The pursuer is responsible, in the first instance, for payment of the fees and outlays of the curator *ad litem* incurred during the period from his appointment until—

(a)   he lodges a minute stating that he does not intend to lodge defences;

(b)   he decides to instruct the lodging of defences or a minute adopting defences already lodged; or

---

[51] r. 33.16(2).

[52] r. 33.16(3).

[53] r. 33.16(4).

[54] r. 33.16(4) and (6).

[55] r. 33.16(7).

[56] r. 33.16(8).

(c) being satisfied after investigation that the defender is not suffering from mental disorder, he is discharged.[57]

The effect of mental disorder on the use of affidavit procedure and the simplified procedure is noted in Chapter 1.[58]

---

[57] r. 33.16(9).
[58] See Chap.1, text accompanying nn. 31 and 53.

CHAPTER 3

THE MERITS

IN an action for divorce the court may upon an application by the pursuer[1] grant decree of divorce, if, but only if, it is established in accordance with section 1(2) of the Divorce (Scotland) Act 1976 that the marriage has broken down irretrievably.[2] There are five ways of establishing irretrievable breakdown, each of which is considered in turn. Some general rules relating to proof of the merits of a divorce action are considered first.

Sufficiency of evidence

Some specialities regarding sufficiency of evidence in divorce actions require mention:

(a)   subject to section 8(4) of the Civil Evidence (Scotland) Act 1988 (as to which, see (b) *infra*), the evidence in an action of divorce establishing the grounds of action must consist of or include evidence other than that of a party to the marriage.[3] The evidence of the parties, therefore, whilst admissible,[4] is always insufficient (except in cases falling within (b)).

(b)   by virtue of section 8(4) of the Civil Evidence (Scotland) Act 1988 and the Evidence in Divorce Actions (Scotland) Order 1989,[5] the foregoing requirement of evidence other than that of a party to the marriage does not apply to actions of divorce in which—

(i)   the action is undefended[6];

---

[1] There is no provision in the ordinary cause rules for a defender to apply for decree of divorce (*cf. Farley* v. *Farley*, 1991 S.L.T. 74).

[2] 1976 Act, s.1(1).

[3] Civil Evidence (Scotland) Act 1988, s.8(3).

[4] Evidence Further Amendment (Scotland) Act 1874, s.2. Note that failure by the defender to lodge defences is not a fact upon which the pursuer may found (*Barr* v. *Barr*, 1939 S.C. 696).

[5] S.I. 1989 No. 582, paras. 2(1) and 3.

[6] For the purpose of the Order, an action is treated as undefended when the defender has not entered appearance or, having entered appearance, has not lodged defences or has withdrawn them—para. 2(2).

(ii) the action is brought in reliance on the facts set out in section 1(2)(*d*) and (*e*) of the Divorce (Scotland) Act 1976;

(iii) there are no children of the marriage under the age of 16 years;

(iv) neither party applies for an order for financial provision on divorce; and

(v) neither party suffers from mental disorder within the meaning of section 1(2) of the Mental Health (Scotland) Act 1984 (*i.e.* mental illness or mental handicap, however caused or manifested).

(c) by virtue of section 3(1) of the Divorce (Scotland) Act 1976, where a decree of separation has been granted in respect of facts which are the same, or substantially the same, as those averred in support of an action for divorce, an extract of that decree lodged in process may be treated as sufficient proof of the facts upon which such decree was granted.

The foregoing does not entitle the court to grant decree of divorce without receiving evidence from the pursuer,[7] for:

"Past conduct that has become spent will not do. . . . There must in every case be a live cause of action. It follows that, while past conduct may suffice, every action must be subject to all such bars, impediments, and defences as are open in all actions of divorce under the existing law."[8]

The pursuer must therefore, in addition to lodging a certified copy initial writ and extract decree of separation, update by way of affidavit or parole evidence the contents thereof (usually by narrating that the parties have neither lived together nor had marital relations since the date upon which decree of separation was granted).

Section 3(1) is not applicable to actions of divorce for adultery (which are separately provided for[9]) and is necessarily of limited value, if any, in relation to two- and five-year actions.[10]

---

[7] 1976 Act, s.3(2).

[8] *Per* Lord Justice-Clerk Aitchison in *Wilson* v. *Wilson*, 1939 S.C. 102 at p. 107.

[9] Law Reform (Miscellaneous Provisions) (Scotland) Act 1968, s.11.

[10] This is because the relevant period of the parties' non-cohabitation in these cases is that immediately preceding the bringing of the action of divorce; in two-year cases there is the added complication that the defender must consent to the granting of decree of divorce.

Burden and standard of proof
The onus of proving irretrievable breakdown of the marriage is of course on the pursuer. It is not for her to prove the absence of any defence to divorce, but, as Clive puts it:

> "Divorce procedure . . . is not purely adversarial. The court can take note of bars to divorce even if not pleaded and is entitled to require full information to be laid before it, where that can reasonably be done, to enable it to discharge its functions. It is not reasonable to expect the pursuer to negate *lenocinium* and collusion. It is, however, reasonable enough to expect the pursuer to say whether there has been cohabitation between the parties after adultery or after the expiry of the two-year period in a divorce for desertion. It is also reasonable enough to expect the pursuer in a five years case to provide information about the financial position of the parties so far as known to him."[11]

The standard of proof required to establish irretrievable breakdown is proof on the balance of probability.[12]

Competency and compellability of witnesses
The rules of competency and compellability of witnesses apply to actions of divorce as to other causes, with the exception that the privilege attached to communications between spouses during the marriage has not in practice been applied in relation to the merits of divorce.[13] (On the other hand, there has been no relaxation in practice of the statutory protection[14] afforded to all witnesses against any question tending to show that he or she has been guilty of adultery.) The parties to an action of divorce are

---

[11] At pp. 443 and 444. In their *Report on Family Law* (Scot. Law Com. No. 135, 1992) the Scottish Law Commission propose an amendment to the Divorce (Scotland) Act 1976 as follows:

"8A. In an action for divorce the court shall not grant decree of divorce if it is satisfied that (whether or not through the collusion of the parties) the pursuer has put forward a false case or the defender has withheld a good defence."

[12] 1976 Act, s.1(6).

[13] Evidence (Scotland) Act 1853, s.3, not applied in *Gallacher* v. *Gallacher*, 1934 S.C. 339, and *Mackay* v. *Mackay*, 1946 S.C. 78.

[14] Evidence Further Amendment (Scotland) Act 1874, s.2. It has been held that where a witness admits adultery on oath by way of an affidavit, such affidavit should disclose *in gremio* that the witness has been warned of his or her right to refuse to answer any question tending to show guilt of adultery—*Cooper* v. *Cooper*, 1987 S.L.T. (Sh.Ct.) 37 (*cf. Sinclair* v. *Sinclair*, 1986 S.L.T. (Sh.Ct.) 54).

competent and probably compellable witnesses.[15] Neither can be compelled in any proceedings to give evidence that marital intercourse did or did not take place between them during any period.[16]

Although it may not strictly be a matter of competency or compellability, the attention of practitioners is drawn to judicial dicta stressing that it is undesirable for the defender to avoid giving evidence in a defended divorce action.[17]

ADULTERY

Irretrievable breakdown is established if:

> "since the date of the marriage the defender has committed adultery" (1976 Act, s.1(2)(*a*)).

Adultery is:

> "voluntary sexual intercourse between a married person and a person of the opposite sex, not being the marriage partner."[18]

Thus one act of adultery is sufficient. How the offended spouse responds to it or perceives it is immaterial.[19] Whether or not the marriage partners were cohabiting at the time is irrelevant. Good faith (*e.g.* committing adultery in the genuine belief that the marriage partner is dead) is not a defence.[20]

Adminicles of evidence relevant to proof of adultery include admissions of adultery,[21] "opportunity plus,"[22] diaries and letters,[23] fathering or mothering a child by a third party[24] and other sexual behaviour.[25]

Irretrievable breakdown is not to be taken to be established if

---

[15] Clive, p. 446.

[16] Law Reform (Miscellaneous Provisions) Act 1949, s.7(2).

[17] *Bird* v. *Bird*, 1931 S.C. 371 at pp. 374 and 375, and *White* v. *White*, 1947 S.L.T. (Notes) 51; see also *Thomson* v. *Thomson*, 1955 S.L.T. (Sh.Ct.) 99.

[18] Clive, p. 402, referring to monogamous marriages. As to adultery and polygamy, see Clive, p. 403.

[19] *Stewart* v. *Stewart*, 1987 S.L.T. (Sh.Ct.) 48 at p. 50.

[20] *Hunter* v. *Hunter*, (1900) 2 F. 774.

[21] See Clive, p. 455.

[22] *Ibid.* p. 463 and *White* v. *White*, 1990 G.W.D. 12–612.

[23] *Ibid.*, pp. 455–458.

[24] *Ibid.*, pp. 458–462.

[25] *Ibid.*, pp. 462–464.

the adultery has been connived at in such a way as to raise the defence of *lenocinium*.[26] The essence of this defence, according to Clive, is:

> "that a spouse who has actively promoted, or who is art and part in, the other spouse's adultery cannot found on that adultery as a ground of divorce."[27]

Irretrievable breakdown is also not to be taken to be established if the adultery has been condoned by the pursuer's cohabitation with the defender in the knowledge or belief that the defender has committed the adultery; and adultery will not be held to have been so condoned by reason only of the fact that after the commission of the adultery the pursuer has continued or resumed cohabitation with the defender, provided that the pursuer has not cohabited with the defender at any time after the end of the period of three months from the date on which cohabitation was continued or resumed with the aforesaid knowledge or belief.[28]

Intimation of an adultery action and of an adultery allegation falls to be made in accordance with rules 33.7 (1)(*b*) and 33.15 (2), respectively.[29]

BEHAVIOUR

Irretrievable breakdown is established if:

> "since the date of the marriage the defender has at any time behaved (whether or not as a result of mental abnormality and whether such behaviour has been active or passive) in such a way that the pursuer cannot reasonably be expected to cohabit with the defender" (1976 Act, s.1(2)(*b*)).

The question as to whether the pursuer can reasonably be expected to cohabit with the defender is a question as to the

---

[26] 1976 Act, s.1(3). The Scottish Law Commission in their *Report on Family Law* (Scot. Law Com. No. 135) propose that s. 1(3) be amended so as to read that irretrievable breakdown is not to be taken to be established if the adultery has been "actively promoted or encouraged by the pursuer."

[27] p. 433. Examples of this bar to divorce are putting one's wife out to prostitution, indulging in wife-swapping and encouraging one's wife to commit adultery in order to obtain evidence for a divorce.

[28] 1976 Act, ss.1(3) and 2(2).

[29] See Chap. 1, text accompanying nn. 11, 12 and 23.

position at the date of proof and the court is entitled to take into account the pursuer's circumstances at that date and the changes that will have occurred in the parties' lives since they separated.[30] Irretrievable breakdown is however only to be taken to be established where the fact that the pursuer cannot reasonably be expected to cohabit with the defender flows, in a causal sense, from the nature of the relevant behaviour of the defender.[31]

Whereas "adultery is based on objective fact and affords a ground for divorce however the offended spouse responds to it or perceives it ... in relation to s.1(2)(b) of the 1976 Act, the effective question is how the offended spouse could reasonably be expected to react to specific behaviour on the part of the other spouse."[32] The more obvious examples of behaviour establishing irretrievable breakdown include habitual abuse of alcohol or drugs, violence directed at the pursuer (including attempted and threatened violence), and extra-marital sexual activity (including sodomy, incest or any homosexual relationship,[33] bestiality and other indecent behaviour, adultery and, depending on the circumstances, behaviour with other members of the opposite sex falling short of adultery[34]). Relevant conduct may be persistent, or cumulative, or (exceptionally) neither: " ... conduct on the part of a defender, by word or act, may be of such a nature that even if there is no risk of a repetition it is so destructive of a marriage relationship as to make it unreasonable to expect the pursuer to cohabit with the defender."[35]

Where the defender has been convicted of a criminal offence upon which the pursuer wishes to found (*e.g.* assault upon her),

---

[30] *Findlay* v. *Findlay*, 1991 S.L.T. 457.

[31] *Ibid. See* also *Knox* v. *Knox*, 1993 S.C.L.R. 381.

[32] *Stewart loc. cit.* (admission of extra-marital "association" after persistent late homecoming justified divorce). See also *McCulloch* v. *McCulloch*, 1987 G.W.D. 19–738.

[33] Where the pursuer alleges sodomy, incest or any homosexual relationship between the defender and another named person, r. 33.8 applies. Rule 33.8(1) requires the pursuer, immediately after expiry of the period of notice, to lodge a motion for an order for intimation to that person or to dispense with such intimation. In terms of r. 33.8 (2), the sheriff in determining the motion may (a) make such order for intimation as he thinks fit; or (b) dispense with intimation; and (c) where he dispenses with intimation, order that the name of that person be deleted from the condescendence of the initial writ. Where intimation is ordered, a copy of the initial writ and an intimation in Form F13 must be intimated to the named person (r. 33.8(3)).

[34] *Stewart, supra.*

[35] *Hastie* v. *Hastie*, 1985 S.L.T. 146 at p. 148 (false accusations of infidelity and of an incestuous association) (*cf. Gray* v. *Gray*, 1991 G.W.D. 8–477).

she may rely upon section 10 of the Law Reform (Miscellaneous Provisions) (Scotland) Act 1968 to establish the commission of the offence. It is improper, it is considered, to aver that a person has been convicted of a criminal offence without first having had sight of an extract conviction.

DESERTION

Irretrievable breakdown is established if:

> "the defender has wilfully and without reasonable cause deserted the pursuer; and during a continuous period of two years immediately succeeding the defender's desertion—
> (i)   there has been no cohabitation between the parties, and
> (ii)   the pursuer has not refused a genuine and reasonable offer by the defender to adhere." (1976 Act, s.1(2)(*c*)).

This provision may be broken down into its component parts as follows:

(a)   The defender has wilfully deserted the pursuer.
This entails the defender's withdrawal from cohabitation with the intention of ending the married life, while the pursuer is willing to continue it.[36]

(b)   The desertion was without reasonable cause.
Adultery committed by the pursuer provides "reasonable cause" for the defender to desert, as does behaviour on her part falling within section 1(2)(*b*). There is a question as to whether the conduct founded on by the defender requires to have been known to him at the time of desertion in order to provide "reasonable cause."[37]

(c)   During a continuous period of two years immediately succeeding the defender's desertion there has been no cohabitation between the parties.[38]
If, after the expiry of the two-year period, the pursuer has resumed cohabitation with the defender and has

---

[36] See, generally, Clive, pp. 415–420.
[37] Fully discussed by Clive, pp. 420–423.
[38] The action must be brought after the expiry of that period (n. 41 *infra*). As to "cohabitation" and the statutory provision affecting the assessment of whether or not the two-year period has been continuous, see nn. 42 to 44 *infra* and accompanying text.

cohabited with the defender at any time after the end of the period of three months from the date on which cohabitation was resumed as aforesaid, irretrievable breakdown will not be taken to have been established.[39]

(d) During the aforesaid two-year period the pursuer has not refused a genuine and reasonable offer by the defender to adhere.

Whether an offer is "genuine and reasonable" will turn on the facts of the particular case; the defender will generally be well-advised not to attach conditions to the offer.[40]

TWO-YEAR AND FIVE-YEAR ACTIONS

Irretrievable breakdown is established if:

> "there has been no cohabitation between the parties at any time during a continuous period of two years after the date of the marriage and immediately preceding the bringing of the action[41] and the defender consents to the granting of decree of divorce" (1976 Act, s.1(2)(*d*));

or:

> "there has been no cohabitation between the parties at any time during a continuous period of five years after the date of the marriage and immediately preceding the bringing of the action."[41] (1976 Act, s.1(2)(*e*)).

In both actions, accordingly, it must be averred and proved that the parties have not cohabited for the requisite period of time.

Section 13(2) of the 1976 Act provides that:

> "the parties to a marriage shall be held to cohabit with one another only when they are in fact living together as man and wife; and 'cohabitation' shall be construed accordingly."[42]

---

[39] 1976 Act, s.2(3).

[40] See, *e.g. Burnett* v. *Burnett*, 1958 S.C. 1 and earlier cases cited by Clive at p. 424.

[41] An action raised before the expiry of the requisite period of non-cohabitation is "manifestly groundless"—*Matthews* v. *Matthews*, 1985 S.L.T. (Sh.Ct.) 68. Conversion of an action, whether for divorce or for separation, to a two-year or five-year action by amendment after the expiry of the requisite period of non-cohabitation is competent—*Duncan* v. *Duncan*, 1986 S.L.T. 17; *Edgar* v. *Edgar*, 1990 S.L.T. (Sh.Ct.) 82 (*cf. Porter* v. *Porter, ibid.*).

[42] The expression "in fact living together as man and wife" is considered in detail by Clive at pp. 429 to 431. At p. 429 he suggests: "Whether a couple are in fact

In considering whether or not a period of non-cohabitation has been continuous no account is to be taken of any period(s) not exceeding six months[43] in all during which the parties cohabited with one another, any such period (or periods) however not counting as part of the period of non-cohabitation.[44]

It should specifically be averred in a two-year case that the defender consents to decree of divorce.

Ordinary cause rules 33.14 and 33.18 provide the machinery for the giving and the withdrawal of consent to the granting of decree of divorce.

The pursuer requires to attach to the copy initial writ served upon the defender a notice in Form F19 and a notice of consent in Form F20.[45] The defender thereafter indicates to the court his consent by giving notice in writing in Form F20 to the sheriff clerk.[46] The evidence of one witness is sufficient for the purpose of establishing that the signature on the notice of consent is that of the defender.[47]

The defender is entitled to withdraw his consent at any time and for any reason. Where the initial writ contains an averment that the defender consents to the grant of decree, he may give notice in writing to the court that he has not consented to decree

---

living together as man and wife is, manifestly, a question of fact.... The question must be approached by applying the statutory words directly to the circumstances of each case. Various factors will be important—the amount and nature of time spent together, living under the same roof, sleeping together, having sexual intercourse together, eating together, having a social life and other leisure activities together, supporting each other, talking to each other, loving each other, sharing resources, sharing household and child-rearing tasks and so on—but, with one apparent exception, none will be conclusive on its own. The one apparent exception is total physical separation for the two- or five-year period. It is only an apparent exception because this factor cannot exist on its own: it necessarily involves an absence of most other relevant factors."

[43] According to Clive, this must mean six *lunar* months (*i.e.* 24 weeks) rather than six *calendar* months (p. 431).

[44] 1976 Act, s.2(4) (applicable to desertion, two-year and five-year cases); if a pursuer intends to found on this provision, that intention should be made clear upon averment—*Edmond* v. *Edmond*, 1971 S.L.T. (Notes) 8 at p. 9.

[45] r. 33.14(1)(*a*)(i). The certificate of service must state which notice or form has been attached in the initial writ—r. 33.14(2).

[46] r. 33.18(1). The defender is free to deliver the notice of consent personally or have an intermediary (*e.g.* the pursuer's solicitor) deliver it—*Taylor* v. *Taylor*, 1988 S.C.L.R. 60.

[47] r. 33.18(2). It has been held that where a lengthy period of time has elapsed since the date of the defender's signature the sheriff has a discretion as to whether or not to treat the consent form as valid—*Donnelly* v. *Donnelly*, 1991 S.L.T. (Sh.Ct.) 9.

being granted or that he withdraws any consent which he has already given.[48] Where he does so, the sheriff clerk must intimate the terms of the letter to the pursuer who is required within 14 days after the date of the intimation, if none of the other facts mentioned in section 1(2) of the Divorce (Scotland) Act 1976 is averred in the initial writ, to lodge a motion for the action to be sisted.[49] If no such motion is lodged, the pursuer shall be deemed to have abandoned the action and the action must be dismissed.[50] If the motion is granted and the sist is not recalled or renewed within a period of six months from the date of the interlocutor granting the sist, the pursuer is deemed to have abandoned the action and the action must be dismissed.[51] In any case where the defender has not given or has withdrawn his consent, it is incompetent or at least inappropriate, it seems, for the court to pronounce any interlocutor in the process, save as already mentioned.[52]

Notwithstanding that irretrievable breakdown has been established in a five-year case, the court is not bound to grant decree if in the opinion of the court the grant of decree of divorce would result in grave financial hardship to the defender.[53] "Hardship" is defined as including the loss of the chance of acquiring any benefit.[54]

In order to enable the court to exercise its discretion in the area, the pursuer in any five-year case should narrate the whole financial circumstances of both parties, whether a financial claim is to be made or not.[55]

The pursuer in a five-year case requires to send with the copy initial writ served upon the defender a notice as nearly as may be in terms of Form F23.[56]

---

[48] r. 33.18(3).
[49] r. 33.18(4) and (5).
[50] r. 33.18(6).
[51] r. 33.18(7).
[52] See *Boyle* v. *Boyle*, 1977 S.L.T. (Notes) 69.
[53] 1976 Act, s.1(5). See *e.g. Nolan* v. *Nolan*, 1979 S.L.T. 293 and *Boyd* v. *Boyd*, 1978 S.L.T. (Notes) 55. The Scottish Law Commission in their *Report on Family Law* (Scot. Law Com. No. 135, 1992) propose the repeal of this subsection, which rests uneasily with the court's powers in the Family Law (Scotland) Act 1985 for the ordering of financial provision (see, especially, Chap. 7, text accompanying n. 84).
[54] *Ibid.*
[55] See text accompanying n. 11 *supra.*
[56] r. 33.14(1)(*b*)(i). The certificate of service must state which notice or form has been attached to the initial writ—r. 33.14(2).

Where the defender's address is unknown in a five-year case, the pursuer must satisfy the court that all reasonable steps have been taken to ascertain it.[57] Averments setting out what steps have been taken should be made.[58]

---

[57] 1976 Act, s.5(6).
[58] r 3.1(6).

CHAPTER 4

PROTECTIVE MEASURES

IN this chapter various measures for the protection of a party's position in an action of divorce are discussed. These range in importance and effect from the accommodation address to matrimonial interdicts and interim exclusion orders.

ACCOMMODATION ADDRESS

Where the pursuer does not wish to disclose her whereabouts to the defender, she may be designed as care of her solicitors in the instance of the initial writ. Use of an accommodation address is however a privilege, for, when a party's true address is not given, he is not properly designed, and accordingly the initial writ is not properly framed.[1]

There are circumstances in which the court will allow the use of an accommodation address (*e.g.* where there would otherwise be a risk of molestation); facts to justify the privilege must however be fully stated in the initial writ.[2] Application may be made to the court by motion to ordain a party using an accommodation address to reveal his or her true address.[3]

MATRIMONIAL INTERDICTS

An interdict is a matrimonial interdict (to which a power of arrest may be attached[4]) if it is:

"an interdict including an interim interdict which—

---

[1] *Doughton* v. *Doughton*, 1958 S.L.T. (Notes) 34.
[2] *Ibid.*
[3] As in *Stein* v. *Stein*, 1936 S.L.T. 103.
[4] Powers of arrest are dealt with in this chapter, *infra*.

(a) restrains or prohibits any conduct of one spouse towards the other spouse or a child of the family, or

(b) prohibits a spouse from entering or remaining in a matrimonial home or in a specified area in the vicinity of the matrimonial home."[5]

The phrase "matrimonial interdict" itself has no content unless applied to an interdict in specific terms; and such interdict, to be classed a "matrimonial interdict," must fall within the category of interdict above-mentioned.[6] A matrimonial interdict may have a common law or a statutory basis.[7] If the former, the terms of the interdict "must be no wider than are necessary to curb the illegal actings complained of, and so precise and clear that the person

---

[5] Matrimonial Homes (Family Protection) (Scotland) Act 1981, s.14(2). *Quaere* whether an interdict preventing removal of a child (*infra*) is a matrimonial interdict. In their *Report on Family Law* (Scot. Law Com. No. 135, 1992) the Scottish Law Commission propose the repeal of s.14 and its substitution by the following:
"14. (1) The court may, on the application of a spouse, grant an interdict, or an interim interdict, (to be known as a 'matrimonial interdict') which—
  (a) restrains or prohibits any conduct of the non-applicant spouse towards the applicant spouse or a child of the family; or
  (b) subject to subsection (2) below, prohibits the non-applicant spouse from entering or remaining in—
    (i) the matrimonial home;
    (ii) any other home or other premises occupied by the applicant spouse;
    (iii) any place of work, or the school attended by any child in the care, of the applicant spouse; or
    (iv) a specified area in the vicinity of any such home, premises, place of work or school.
(2) If the non-applicant spouse is entitled, or permitted by a third party, to occupy the matrimonial home, or has occupancy rights in it, the court shall not grant a matrimonial interdict prohibiting that spouse from entering, or remaining in, that home or a specified area in its vicinity unless the interdict is ancillary to an exclusion order or (as the case may be) to a refusal by the court of leave to exercise occupancy rights in the circumstances mentioned in section 1(3) of this Act.
(3) In the foregoing provisions of this section . . .—
'applicant spouse' means the spouse who applied for the interdict;
'non-applicant spouse' shall be construed accordingly;
'spouse' includes former spouse.
(4) It shall be competent for the court to entertain an application for a matrimonial interdict, whether or not the spouses concerned are living together as husband and wife."
[6] *McKenna* v. *McKenna*, 1984 S.L.T. (Sh.Ct.) 92 at p. 95.
[7] As to the latter, see Interim Exclusion Orders, *infra*.

interdicted is left in no doubt what he is forbidden to do"[8]; must be "sharply defined and related specifically to the particular risks which justify its grant"[9]; must not be so framed as to prevent the exercise of undoubted legal rights[10]; and must be justified by the applicant's pleadings.[11]

Where there is no information of a wrong actually being committed by the defender against the pursuer, there must be reasonable apprehension that the defender may, in the future, do the illegal acts which the pursuer seeks to have him restrained from doing in her crave.[12] The court must be "satisfied that the pursuer, unless interdict is granted, is likely to be exposed, without other adequate protection, to conduct on the part of the defender which will put her at risk or in fear, alarm, or distress."[9]

In any application for perpetual interdict, whether or not the action is defended, it is the duty of the court to exercise a sound judicial discretion in deciding whether interdict should be granted; and such grant can only be made on strong or at least reasonable grounds.[13] It is competent for a sheriff to grant a matrimonial interdict preventing the commission of an unlawful act outwith his territorial jurisdiction.[14]

When an interim interdict in a divorce process is claimed to have been breached, a minute may be lodged containing detailed averments in support of a crave for the court to ordain the defender to appear at the bar to explain his actings.[15] A breach of

---

[8] *Per* Lord President Emslie in *Murdoch* v. *Murdoch,* 1973 S.L.T. (Notes) 13 at p. 13. In *McKenna, supra,* it was considered reasonable to protect the pursuer against the possibility that the defender would seek him out at his home.

[9] *Per* Lord President Emslie in *Murdoch, loc. cit., supra.*

[10] *Tattersall* v. *Tattersall,* 1983 S.L.T. 506, wherein the legal rights in question were those of the tenant in respect of possession of the property. An interdict at common law against a non-entitled spouse seeking to enter the matrimonial home without leave of the court would, it is thought, be competent (*cf. MacLure* v. *MacLure,* 1911 S.C. 200). An interdict at common law against an entitled spouse seeking to prevent a non-entitled spouse from continuing to occupy the matrimonial home is competent (*Mazur* v. *Mazur,* 1990 G.W.D. 35–2017). An interdict at common law preventing removal of furniture and plenishings from the matrimonial home has been held to be competent (*Welsh* v. *Welsh,* 1987 S.L.T. (Sh.Ct.) 30).

[11] See, *e.g. McKenna, supra.* Any course of conduct and incident or incidents founded upon should be averred in detail.

[12] *Bailey* v. *Bailey,* 1987 S.C.L.R. 1, at p. 4.

[13] *Bailey, loc. cit.* (see also *Gunn* v. *Gunn,* 1955 S.L.T. (Notes) 69).

[14] *McKenna, supra* (*cf. Calder Chemicals Ltd.* v. *Brunton,* 1984 S.L.T. (Sh.Ct.) 96).

[15] See *Gribben* v. *Gribben,* 1976 S.L.T. 266.

interdict constitutes a contempt of court which may lead to punishment, and it is necessary in the interests of fairness that the alleged contempt should be clearly and distinctly averred and that the proceedings for contempt be confined to the averments.[16]

Such a minute may only be presented with the concurrence of the procurator fiscal concerned with any criminal proceedings which may be taken as a result of the actings in question.[17] It is understood that consent will not be forthcoming if the matter is to be the subject of such proceedings. If the alleged breach is denied, answers may be ordered and a proof held. The standard of proof is proof beyond reasonable doubt.[18] Proceedings for breach of interdict are civil proceedings to which section 1 of the Civil Evidence (Scotland) Act 1988 applies.[19] If the breach is admitted or proved, the defender is liable to punishment by fine or imprisonment.[20] The sheriff's disposal may be appealed to the Court of Session (but not to the sheriff principal).[21]

Where perpetual interdict is claimed to have been breached, procedure is by way of initial writ.[22]

POWERS OF ARREST

A power of arrest entitles a police officer to arrest without warrant a spouse whom he has reasonable cause to suspect is in breach of a matrimonial interdict.[23] The court must attach a power of arrest, when asked, where the matrimonial interdict is ancillary to an exclusion order, or an interim exclusion order.[24] The court must also do so, when asked, in relation to any other matrimonial interdict, subject to two provisos:

---

[16] *Byrne* v. *Ross*, 1993 S.L.T. 307.
[17] *Gribben, cit. supra.* Once the procurator fiscal has indicated that he does not intend to intervene, it is not necessary to intimate any adjustments or amendments to the minute regarding other incidents which are all part of the same course of conduct—*Byrne*, at p. 310.
[18] *Gribben, cit. supra.*
[19] *Byrne, cit. supra.*
[20] *Forbes* v. *Forbes*, 1993 G.W.D. 12–849. Note the observation in *Forbes* that it was proper not to hear any submissions from the minuter on the matter of penalty.
[21] See Dobie, *Sheriff Court Practice*, p. 509.
[22] e.g. *Forbes, cit. supra.*
[23] 1981 Act, s.15(3). Police powers and procedure following arrest are governed by ss.16 and 17 of the Act.
[24] 1981 Act, s.15(1)(a).

(1)   the non-applicant spouse must have had the opportunity of being heard by or represented before the court[25]; and

(2)   the court need not do so where it appears to the court that in all the circumstances of the case such a power is unnecessary.[26]

An application for an order attaching a power of arrest, if made after the application for matrimonial interdict, must be made by motion intimated to the non-applicant spouse.[27]

A power of arrest has no effect unless and until the interdict together with the attached power of arrest is served on the non-applicant spouse.[28] The applicant spouse requires as soon as possible after such service on the non-applicant spouse to ensure that there is delivered to the chief constable of the police area in which the matrimonial home is situated (and also to his counterpart in the police area in which the applicant spouse resides, if different) the following:

(i)   a copy of the application for the interdict;

(ii) a copy of the interlocutor granting the interdict; and

(iii) a certificate of service of the interdict[29];

and, where the application to attach the power of arrest to the interdict was made after the interdict was granted,

(i)   a copy of the application to attach the power of arrest to the interdict;

(ii) a copy of the interlocutor granting that application; and

(iii) a certificate of service of the interdict together with the attached power of arrest[30];

---

[25] Intimation of the motion falls to be given in terms of r. 33.69(2) (see n. 27 *infra*) if it is made after application for matrimonial interdict—r. 33.69(1)(*d*).

[26] *Ibid.*, s.15(1)(*b*). The power might be considered unnecessary if a long time has elapsed without incident since the interdict was served upon the non-applicant spouse. Since the procedure outlined in the text accompanying nn. 15–20 *supra* for the enforcement of interim interdicts may be time-consuming, practitioners should consider applying for the attachment of the power as a matter of course. In their *Report on Family Law* (Scot. Law Com. No. 135, 1992) the Scottish Law Commission propose substituting for the words "it appears to the court" the words "the court is satisfied by the non-applicant spouse".

[27] r. 33.69(1)(*d*) and (2)(*a*). Otherwise, the application is made by a crave in the initial writ or defences—rr. 33.67(1)(*b*) and 33.34(1)(*c*)(iii) and (2)(*b*)(i).

[28] 1981 Act, s.15(2), as amended by the Law Reform (Miscellaneous Provisions) (Scotland) Act 1990, s.64(*a*).

[29] *Ibid.*, s.15(4).

[30] *Ibid.*, s.15(4), as amended by the Law Reform (Miscellaneous Provisions) (Scotland) Act 1990, s.64(*b*).

and must thereafter lodge in process a certificate of delivery in Form F30.[31]

Unless previously recalled, a power of arrest ceases to have effect upon the termination of the marriage.[32] Where the power of arrest ceases to have effect by reason of variation or recall of the matrimonial interdict, the spouse who applied for the variation or recall must carry out the same procedure with respect to a copy of the application for variation or recall and of the interlocutor granting the application, and must thereafter lodge in process a certificate of delivery in Form F30.[33] The foregoing must also be done where the power of arrest ceases to have effect by reason of decree of divorce being granted, the procedure being carried out by the applicant spouse.[34]

Application to the sheriff for recall of a power of arrest requires to be made by minute intimated to the other spouse.[35]

INTERIM EXCLUSION ORDERS[36]

Where there is an entitled and a non-entitled spouse,[37] or where both spouses are entitled, or permitted by a third party, to occupy

---

[31] r. 33.72(1).

[32] 1981 Act, s.15(2). In their *Report on Family Law* (Scot. Law Com. No. 135, 1992) the Scottish Law Commission propose amending s.15(2) so as to provide that a power of arrest ceases to have effect on the expiry of a period of three years commencing with the date on which the power was granted unless it has been recalled or, on cause shown, renewed within that period.

[33] r. 33.72(1).

[34] r. 33.72(2).

[35] r. 33.70(1)(*b*) and (2)(*a*).

[36] "Interim exclusion order" is not a term found in the 1981 Act; it is used here to denote an interim order granted in terms of s.4(6) of the Act. Since exclusion orders cease to have effect upon termination of the marriage (1981 Act, s.5(1)(*a*)), it seems appropriate when discussing the exclusion of a party to a divorce action from a matrimonial home to concentrate upon such orders *ad interim*. Different considerations apply in respect of the court's power, on or after granting decree of divorce, to grant an incidental order excluding a party to the marriage from occupation of a matrimonial home (as to which, see Chap. 7, (second) n. 8 and accompanying text). The tests applicable to the making of exclusion orders (text accompanying nn. 42 to 46) apply also to the making of interim exclusion orders (*Bell* v. *Bell*, 1983 S.L.T. 224 and *Ward* v. *Ward*, 1983 S.L.T. 472).

[37] A "non-entitled spouse" is a spouse who, apart from the provisions of the 1981 Act, is not entitled, or permitted by a third party, to occupy a matrimonial home: such a spouse has the right (a) if in occupation, to continue to occupy the matrimonial home, together with any child of the family, and (b) if not in

a matrimonial home,[38] either spouse, whether or not in occupation at the time of the application, may apply to the court for an order (an "exclusion order") suspending the occupancy rights of the other spouse in a matrimonial home.[39] Application for an interim exclusion order requires to be made by motion.[40] An interim order may only be made if the non-applicant spouse

occupation, with leave of the court to enter into and occupy the matrimonial home, together with any child of the family—1981 Act, s.1(1), (1A) and (3), as amended by the Law Reform (Miscellaneous Provisions) (Scotland) Act 1985, s.13(2) and (3). In their *Report on Family Law* (Scot. Law Com. No. 135, 1992), the Scottish Law Commission propose an amendment to s.1 so as to add the following subsection:

"(7) If an entitled spouse and a non-entitled spouse have been living apart from each other for a continuous period of two years and the non-entitled spouse has not occupied the matrimonial home at any time during that period, the occupancy rights of the non-entitled spouse in the home shall be extinguished at the end of that period."

[38] "Matrimonial home" means any house, caravan, houseboat or other structure, which has been provided or has been made available by one or both of the spouses as, or has become, a family residence and includes any garden or other ground or building attached to, and usually occupied with, or otherwise required for the amenity or convenience of, the house, caravan, houseboat or other structure but does not include a residence provided or made available by one spouse for that spouse to reside in, whether with any child of the family or not, separately from the other spouse—1981 Act, s.22, as amended by the Law Reform (Miscellaneous Provisions) (Scotland) Act 1985, s.13(10). Thus if spouses A and B separate, and A acquires a residence for herself (with or without any children of the marriage), B has no occupancy rights with respect to that residence unless and until invited to live there by A. In their *Report on Family Law* (Scot. Law Com. No. 135, 1992) the Scottish Law Commission propose amending the definition of "matrimonial home" so as to mean:

"any house, caravan, houseboat or other structure which has been provided or has been made available by one or both of the spouses as, or has become, a family residence and includes any garden or other ground or building usually occupied with, or otherwise required for the amenity or convenience of, the house, caravan, houseboat or other structure but does not include a residence provided or made available by anyone for one spouse to reside in, whether with any child of the family or not, separately from the other spouse and if the tenancy of a matrimonial home is transferred from one spouse to the other by agreement or under any enactment in order that the home may become the residence of the transferee separately from the other spouse, the residence shall not be a matrimonial home after the transfer."

[39] 1981 Act, s.4(1), as amended by the Law Reform (Miscellaneous Provisions) (Scotland) Act 1985, s.13(5).

[40] r. 33.69(1)(*b*). Since interim exclusion orders can only be granted "pending the making of an exclusion order" (s.4(6)), the latter should be craved (in the initial writ or in defences, as the case may be—rr. 33.67(1)(*b*) and 33.34(1)(*c*)(iii) and (2) (*b*)(i)).

has been afforded an opportunity of being heard by or represented before the court.[41] The court requires to make the order—

> "if it appears to the court that the making of the order is necessary for the protection of the applicant or any child of the family[42] from any conduct or threatened or reasonably apprehended conduct[43] of the non-applicant spouse which is or would be injurious to the physical or mental health of the applicant or child."[44]

The court must not however make the order:

> "If it appears to the court that the making of the order would be unjustified or unreasonable ... having regard to all the circumstances of the case including ... [45]
>
> (a)   the conduct of the spouses in relation to each other and otherwise;
> (b)   the respective needs and financial resources of the spouses;
> (c)   the needs of any child of the family;
> (d)   the extent (if any) to which the matrimonial home is used in connection with a trade, business or profession of either spouse ...
> (e)   whether the entitled spouse offers or has offered to make available to the non-entitled spouse any suitable alternative accommodation; and

---

[41] 1981 Act, s.4 (6). Failure to intimate the motion for an interim exclusion order to the non-applicant spouse precludes the sheriff from granting it (*Nelson* v. *Nelson*, 1988 S.L.T. (Sh.Ct.) 26). The non-applicant spouse should ordinarily be given an opportunity to lodge affidavits (*Armitage* v. *Armitage*, 1993 S.C.L.R. 173). Rule 33.69 (2) requires intimation of the motion also to be given, where the entitled spouse is a tenant or occupies the matrimonial home by the permission of a third party, to the landlord or third party, as the case may be; and, in any event, to any other person to whom intimation is required by the sheriff to be made.

[42] "Child of the family" includes any child or grandchild of either spouse, and any person who has been brought up or accepted by either spouse as if he or she were a child of that spouse, whatever the age of such a child, grandchild or person may be—*ibid.*, s.22.

[43] As to "conduct" see *Matheson* v. *Matheson*, 1986 S.L.T. (Sh.Ct.) 2 and *Anderson* v. *Anderson*, 1993 G.W.D. 35-2258. The fact that the parties are not at the time of the motion living together is not a bar to the obtaining of an order (*Brown* v. *Brown*, 1985 S.L.T. 376), even where they have been separated for a lengthy period (*Millar* v. *Millar*, 1991 S.C.L.R. 649); but see n.37, *supra*.

[44] 1981 Act, s.4(2). The court does not require, before granting an interim exclusion order, to be satisfied that the applicant spouse would be in immediate danger of suffering irreparable harm (*McCafferty* v. *McCafferty*, 1986 S.L.T. 650 at p. 652).

[45] *Ibid.*, s.4(3).

(f) where the matrimonial home is or is part of an agricultural holding ... , or is let, or is a home in respect of which possession of which is given, to the non-applicant spouse or to both spouses by an employer as an incident of employment, subject to a requirement of residence [therein] ... , that requirement and the likely consequences of the exclusion of the non-applicant spouse from the matrimonial home."[46]

The court has a discretion as to whether or not to make an interim exclusion order; an appellate court could only interfere with any decision taken in exercise of this discretion if it were to be satisfied that the judge of first instance had misdirected himself and had erred in law, or, if he had applied the correct test, that he had reached an unwarranted conclusion.[47] If it appears to the court that an interim interdict (with or without the attachment of a power of arrest, as the case may be) is providing or would provide adequate protection to the applicant spouse, an interim exclusion order will not be granted.[48] The court cannot be satisfied that the making of the order is necessary on the basis of *ex parte* statements alone: there must be "sufficient material [for the court] to be satisfied on a prima facie basis that the pursuer required the protection of such an order."[49] Appropriate "material" includes the following:

---

[46] 1981 Act, ss.3(3) and 4(3).

[47] *McCafferty, supra.* See also *Bell, supra, Brown, supra,* and *Coster* v. *Coster,* 1992 S.C.L.R. 210. An appeal can competently be taken without leave of the sheriff against the award of an interim exclusion order only where an ancillary interim interdict has also been granted (*Oliver* v. *Oliver,* 1989 S.L.T. (Sh.Ct.) 1). Failure by the defender to lodge a notice of intention to defend does not mean he has no locus to appeal (*Nelson, supra*). An interim exclusion order is an exception to the general rule that the effect of an appeal is to sist execution on a decree (*Orr* v. *Orr,* 1989 G.W.D. 12–506).

[48] *Bell, supra.* If the sheriff has applied the correct test and taken into account all relevant factors in granting an interim exclusion order, failure on his part to state that an interim matrimonial interdict preventing molestation would be insufficient to protect the applicant spouse would seem not to justify recall of the order by the appellate court: *Brown, supra* (*cf. Colagiacomo* v. *Colagiacomo, infra,* at p. 561). See also *Ward, supra,* for an illustration of circumstances in which means other than an interim exclusion order would be unlikely to secure the desired degree of protection (drink-related course of conduct over a long period).

[49] *Per* Lord President Emslie in *Ward, supra,* at p. 475. The court in *Ward* relied on material presented in an independent report ordered by the court in connection with a dispute between the parties over custody of their children. Alternatively, the court may order a preliminary proof, as was done in *Bowman* v. *Bowman* (Lord Grieve, February 24, 1984, unreported) and *Assar* v. *Assar,* 1994 G.W.D. 2-102 (on minute and answers).

(i)   Affidavits[50];
(ii)   Extract convictions (where relevant);
(iii) Medical reports.

What quantity and quality of material is sufficient will depend on the circumstances of each case.[51]

In making an interim exclusion order the court *must*, on the application of the applicant spouse:

(i)   grant an interdict prohibiting the non-applicant spouse from entering the matrimonial home without the express permission of the applicant[52];

(ii)   grant a warrant for the summary ejection of the non-applicant spouse from the matrimonial home, unless the non-applicant spouse satisfies the court that it is unnecessary to grant such a warrant[53]; and

(iii) grant an interdict prohibiting the removal by the non-applicant spouse, except with the written consent of the applicant or by a further order of the court, of any furniture and plenishings in the matrimonial home, unless the non-applicant spouse satisfies the court that it is unnecessary to grant such an interdict.[54]

In making an interim exclusion order the court *may*:

(a)   grant an interdict prohibiting the non-applicant spouse from entering or remaining in a specified area in the vicinity of the matrimonial home[55];

(b)   where the warrant for the summary ejection of the non-applicant spouse has been granted in his or her absence, give directions as to the preservation of the non-applicant spouse's goods and effects which remain in the matrimonial home[56];

---

[50] r. 33.27.

[51] See *e.g. Colagiacomo* v. *Colagiacomo*, 1983 S.L.T. 559; *Boyle* v. *Boyle*, 1986 S.L.T. 656; *Coster, supra.*

[52] 1981 Act, s.4(4)(*b*).

[53] *Ibid.*, s.4(4)(*a*). See, *e.g.*, *Mather* v. *Mather*, 1987 S.L.T. 565 (interim exclusion order granted but suspended for three months to allow husband to find alternative accommodation).

[54] *Ibid.*, s.4(4)(*c*). "Furniture and plenishings" means any article situated in a matrimonial home which (a) is owned or hired by either spouse or is being acquired by either spouse under a hire-purchase agreement or conditional sale agreement; and (b) is reasonably necessary to enable the home to be used as a family residence, but does not include any vehicle, caravan, houseboat or other structure as is mentioned in the definition of "matrimonial home" (n. 38, *supra*).

[55] *Ibid.*, s.4(5)(*a*).

[56] *Ibid.*, s.4(5)(*b*).

(c) on the application of either spouse, make the interim exclusion order, or the warrant or interdict mentioned in (i), (ii), (iii) or (a) *supra,* subject to such terms and conditions as the court may prescribe[57]; and

(d) on the application of either spouse, make such other order as it may consider necessary for the proper enforcement of any of the foregoing orders ((i) to (iii) and (a) to (c) inclusive).[58]

Ordinary cause rule 33.70 requires applications for variation or recall of any order suspending occupancy rights to be made by minute intimated: (a) to the other spouse; (b) where the entitled spouse is a tenant or occupies the matrimonial home by the permission of a third party, to the landlord or third party, as the case may be; and (c) to any other person to whom intimation is ordered by the sheriff to be made.[59]

ORDERS RESTRICTING REMOVAL OF CHILDREN

Section 35(3) of the Family Law Act 1986 enables the court in a divorce action to grant interdict or interim interdict prohibiting the removal of a child from the United Kingdom or any part thereof,[60] or out of the control of the person in whose custody the child is.[61] The court may order the surrender of any United Kingdom passport issued to or containing particulars of the child.[62]

---

[57] *Ibid.,* s.4(5)(c).

[58] *Ibid.,* s.4(5)(d).

[59] r. 33.70(1)(a) and (2).

[60] Any such interdict or interim interdict automatically has effect in the rest of the United Kingdom—s.36.

[61] s.35(3)(a) enables the order to be made at any time after the commencement of the proceedings, being proceedings in connection with which the court would have jurisdiction to make a custody order relative to the child. Proceedings are held to commence when the warrant of citation is signed—s.35(5)(b). The order may be applied for by any party to the proceedings, the guardian of the child concerned, and any other person who has or wishes to obtain the custody or care of the child—s.35(4). An application by a party to the action requires to be made by motion (r. 33.24(1)(a)) and by any other person by minute (r.33.24(1)(b)). The application need not be served or intimated (r. 33.24(2)). As to applications under s.23(2) of the Child Abduction and Custody Act 1985, see r. 33.24(3).

[62] s. 37(1).

ORDERS RELATING TO AVOIDANCE TRANSACTIONS

Where an application for an order for financial provision, or for variation or recall of such order, has been made in a divorce action, the party making the claim may, not later than one year from the date of the disposal of the claim, apply[63] to the court for an order—

    (i) setting aside[64] or varying any transfer of, or transaction involving, property effected by the other party not more than five years before the date of the making of the claim; or

    (ii) interdicting the other party from effecting any such transfer or transaction.[65]

If the court is satisfied that the transfer or transaction had the effect of, or is likely to have the effect of, defeating in whole or in part the applicant's claim, it may make the order applied for or such other order as it thinks fit.[66] The court may include in the order such terms and conditions as it thinks fit and may make any ancillary order which it considers expedient to ensure that the order is effective.[67]

The order must not prejudice any rights of a third party in or to the property where that third party:

    (a) has in good faith acquired the property or any of it or any rights in relation to it for value; or

    (b) derives title to such property or rights from any person who has done so.[68]

Intimation therefore requires to be given in accordance with rules 33.7 (1)(*j*) and 33.15 (2).[69]

---

[63] Application must be made by a crave in the initial writ or defences, as the case may be, except that an application after final decree requires to be made by minute in the process of the action to which the application relates—rr. 33.48(1) (*a*) and (2)(*c*) and 33.52(*b*) or r. 33.53(1) and (2).

[64] The power to "set aside" a transaction implies a power to reduce a writing or deed by which the transaction is effected—*Hernandez-Cimorra* v. *Hernandez-Cimorra*, 1992 S.C.L.R. 611. (*Cf. Harris* v. *Harris*, 1988 S.L.T. 101).

[65] Family Law (Scotland) Act 1985, s.18(1).

[66] *Ibid.*, s.18(2).

[67] *Ibid.*, s.18(4).

[68] *Ibid.*, s.18(3). (As to onus, *cf. Leslie* v. *Leslie*, 1983 S.L.T. 186 and 1987 S.L.T. 232).

[69] See Chap. 1, text accompanying nn. 20 and 23.

INHIBITION AND ARRESTMENT ON THE DEPENDENCE

Circumstances may arise in actions of divorce where a financial claim is being made by one spouse against the other in which some security for the claim would be desirable. Inhibition and arrestment on the dependence of the action may be very effective remedies for this purpose. They have been described by the Scottish Law Commission as follows:

"Inhibition is a procedure whereby the defender in an action can be prevented, pending the disposal of the action, from disposing of his heritable property. Arrestment on the dependence is a procedure whereby a third party holding moveable property for the defender or owing money to the defender can be prevented from parting with the property or money pending the disposal of the action."[70]

Where a claim for aliment or for an order for financial provision has been made, the sheriff has power, on cause shown,[71] to grant warrant for arrestment on the dependence of the action in which the claim is made and, if he thinks fit, to limit the arrestment to any particular property or to funds not exceeding a specified value.[72]

Application for a warrant for inhibition requires to be made to the Court of Session, that court having power, on cause shown, to grant such warrant and, if it thinks fit, to limit the inhibition to any particular property.[73] Inhibition has been judicially observed to be a more effective and more suitable method of protection than interdict against the disposal of a heritable property.[74]

---

[70] *Report on Aliment and Financial Provision* (Scot. Law Com. No. 67), para. 3–152.

[71] Such would include where the defender is verging on insolvency (as to which, see *Pow* v. *Pow*, 1987 S.L.T. 127), or is outside Scotland, or is about to decamp, or is depleting his assets to defeat the pursuer's claim—Scot. Law Com., *loc. cit.*

[72] Family Law (Scotland) Act 1985, s.19(1) and (2). As to intimation of applications for such warrant, *cf. Stancroft Securities Ltd.* v. *McDowall*, 1990 S.L.T. 746.

[73] 1985 Act, s.19(1) and (2). Paragraph 2 of the Court of Session Practice Note No. 6 of 1991 provides that an application for warrant to inhibit made by way of Bill for letters of inhibition shall be placed before a Lord Ordinary in chambers and the Lord Ordinary may, after hearing counsel or solicitor for the applicant, authorise the fiat to be granted or may refuse the same. For an illustration of circumstances in which the court's power would not be exercised, see *Thom* v. *Thom*, 1990 S.C.L.R. 800.

[74] *Per* Lord Maxwell in *Wilson* v. *Wilson*, 1981 S.L.T. 101 at p. 102.

CHAPTER 5

PROPERTY ORDERS

THE sheriff is empowered by statute[1] to make various orders, described in this chapter as "property orders," relative to a matrimonial home.[2] In addition to exclusion orders and related remedies (considered in Chapter 4), these include:

(1) an order for the authorisation of a non-entitled spouse to carry out non-essential repairs and improvements in relation to a matrimonial home[3];

(2) orders apportioning between spouses certain expenditure relating to a matrimonial home[4];

(3) orders regulating the spouses' right of occupancy in a matrimonial home[5];

(4) an order dispensing with the consent of a non-entitled spouse to a dealing relating to a matrimonial home[6]; and

(5) an order transferring the tenancy of a matrimonial home from one spouse to the other or, where the spouses are joint or common tenants, vesting the tenancy in one spouse solely.[7]

These orders are of differing significance in the context of actions of divorce; it suffices for present purposes to consider orders under heads (3), (4) and (5).

ORDERS REGULATING OCCUPANCY RIGHTS

Section 3(3) of the Matrimonial Homes (Family Protection) (Scotland) Act 1981 provides for the granting of certain orders

---

[1] The Matrimonial Homes (Family Protection) (Scotland) Act 1981 and the Family Law (Scotland) Act 1985.

[2] Orders introduced by the 1985 Act relative to *any* property of the parties are noted in Chap. 7.

[3] 1981 Act, s.2(1)(*e*) and (4)(*a*).

[4] *Ibid.*, s.2(3), (4)(*b*) and (5)(*b*).

[5] *Ibid.*, s.3.

[6] *Ibid*, s 7.

[7] *Ibid.*, s.13.

concerning spouses' occupancy rights as follows:
  (i)   declaring the occupancy rights of the applicant spouse;
  (ii) enforcing the occupancy rights of the applicant spouse;
  (iii) restricting the occupancy rights of the non-applicant spouse;
  (iv) regulating the exercise by either spouse of his or her occupancy rights;
  (v)   protecting the occupancy rights of the applicant spouse in relation to the other spouse; and
  (vi) granting to a spouse with occupancy rights the possession or use of furniture and plenishings in a matrimonial home owned, hired or being acquired by the other spouse.[8]

An order in category (i) must be granted if it appears to the court that the application relates to a matrimonial home.[9] The court may in terms of section 3(3) make such order relating to an application[10] within the remaining categories as appears to it to be just and reasonable having regard to all the circumstances of the case, including the matters specified in paragraphs (*a*) to (*e*) of the provision, except that no such order may be made if it appears that the effect of the order would be to exclude the non-applicant spouse from the matrimonial home.[11]

Since the granting of decree of divorce automatically terminates occupancy rights,[12] the criteria for the making of interim orders regulating such rights are of greater practical significance for present purposes. These criteria are "necessity" and "expediency", the court being empowered to make such interim order as it may consider necessary or expedient in relation to—

---

[8] *Ibid.*, s.3(1) and (2).
[9] *Ibid.*, s.3(3), subject to s.1(2) (as to which, see *Murphy* v. *Murphy*, 1992 S.C.L.R. 62). Such an order is accordingly appropriately craved where there is any question as to whether or not any particular property is a matrimonial home. There is a suggestion in *Welsh* v. *Welsh*, 1987 S.L.T. (Sh.Ct.) 30 (at p. 32) that such declarator must be obtained before an order in terms of s.3(2) (category (vi)) or s.3(4) (interim order) of the Act can be sought. This appears to depend on the proposition that a spouse does not have occupancy rights unless the court has pronounced decree of declarator to that effect.
[10] An application by a pursuer or a defender must be made by a crave in the initial writ or in defences, as the case may be (rr. 33.67(1)(*b*) and 33.34(1)(*c*)(iii) and (2)(*b*)(i)), intimated in accordance with rr. 33.7(1)(*k*) and 33.15(2) (see Chap. 1, text accompanying nn. 21 and 23).
[11] 1981 Act, s.3(5). (Paras. (*a*) to (*e*) of s.3(3) are set forth in Chap. 4, part of text accompanying n. 46).
[12] This is implicit in the scheme of the Act; subject to s.18, only "spouses" may have occupancy rights; *cf.* s.1.

(a) the residence of either spouse in the home to which the application relates;
(b) the personal effects of either spouse or of any child of the family; or
(c) the furniture and plenishings.[13]

An interim order may only be made if the non-applicant spouse has had an opportunity of being heard by or represented before the court.[14] Application for an interim order must be made by motion.[15] The court may vary or recall an order regulating occupancy rights upon an application therefor made by minute.[16]

Section 14(2) of the Family Law (Scotland) Act 1985 empowers the sheriff, on or after the granting of decree of divorce, to make an incidental order regulating the occupation of the matrimonial home or the use of furniture and plenishings therein or regulating liability, as between the parties, for outgoings in respect of the matrimonial home or furniture or plenishings therein.[17]

ORDERS DISPENSING WITH CONSENT TO DEALING

A non-entitled spouse's occupancy rights are unaffected by any dealing (*e.g.* sale) by the entitled spouse relating to a matrimonial home, except where *inter alia* the non-entitled spouse gives consent thereto.[18] Because occupancy rights depend on there being a subsisting marriage, an entitled spouse with time to await an application for and the granting of decree of divorce need not concern himself to seek that consent. Where however consent is more urgently required and is not forthcoming, the entitled

---

[13] 1981 Act, s.3(4). Note that in terms of s.3(4) an interim order may only be made pending the making of the order under s.3(3), which should therefore be applied for. Illustrations of craves for some such orders are to be found in App. I.

[14] *Ibid.*

[15] r. 33.69(1)(*a*). Intimation of the motion requires to be made to the non-applicant spouse and if the entitled spouse is a tenant or occupies the matrimonial home by the permission of a third party to the landlord or third party, as the case may be—r. 33.69(2).

[16] 1981 Act s.5 and r. 33.70(1)(*a*). Intimation requires to be made in accordance with the preceding footnote.

[17] s.14(2)(*d*) and (*e*) and (3) (as to which, see Chap. 7).

[18] 1981 Act, s.6(1) and (3)(*a*)(i); other exceptions are to be seen in s.6(3).

spouse may apply[19] for an order dispensing with the non-entitled spouse's consent to a "dealing which has taken place or a proposed dealing."[20]

Such an order may be granted if the consent has been unreasonably withheld.[21] The onus is on the applicant spouse to show that consent is being unreasonably withheld.[22] The court in considering whether to make the order must have regard to all the circumstances of the case, including the matters specified in paragraphs (*a*) to (*e*) of section 3(3),[23] except that consent is taken to have been unreasonably withheld where it appears to the court that—

(a)   the non-entitled spouse has led the entitled spouse to believe that such consent would be given and that the non-entitled spouse would not be prejudiced by any change in the circumstances of the case since such apparent consent was given, or

---

[19] Application is by motion intimated to the other spouse and any other person to whom intimation is ordered to be made—r. 33.(1)(*c*) and (2)(*a*) and (*c*). As to procedure where relevant and material facts are disputed, see *Longmuir* v. *Longmuir*, 1985 S.L.T. (Sh.Ct.) 33 at p. 36.

[20] *Ibid.*, s.7(1). " 'A proposed dealing' requires that a stage of negotiations has been reached in which proposals in regard to price and other conditions are being discussed" (*per* Sheriff Principal Gillies in *Fyfe* v. *Fyfe*, 1987 S.L.T. (Sh.Ct.) 38 at p. 41). See also *Dunsmore* v. *Dunsmore*, 1986 S.L.T. (Sh.Ct.) 9 at p. 10. In their *Report on Family Law* (Scot. Law Com. No. 135, 1992) the Scottish Law Commission propose adding the following subsections to s.7:

"(3A) Notwithstanding that negotiations have not yet been started or concluded in relation to a proposed dealing, the court may make an order under subsection (1) above but subject to the dealing consisting of—

(a)   a sale which is for a price not less than an amount specified in the order and which is concluded within such time after the making of the order as may be specified therein;

(b)   the grant of a heritable security for a loan of not more than an amount specified in the order and to be executed within such time after the making of the order as may be specified therein.

(3B) If the court declines to make an order under this section, it may make occupation of the matrimonial home by the non-entitled spouse subject to the non-entitled spouse making payment or payments to the owner of the home, and subject to such other conditions, in respect of the occupancy as the court may specify."

[21] *Ibid.*, s.7(1)(*a*); it may also be granted if consent cannot be given by reason of physical or mental disability or where the non-entitled spouse cannot be found after reasonable steps have been taken to trace him or her, or where he or she is a minor (*ibid.*, s.7(1)(*b*)–(*d*)).

[22] *Hall* v. *Hall*, 1987 S.L.T. (Sh.Ct.) 15.

[23] *Ibid.*, s.7(3). (Paras. (*a*) to (*e*) are set forth in Chap. 4, part of text accompanying n. 46).

(b)   that the entitled spouse has, having taken all reasonable steps to do so, been unable to obtain an answer to a request for consent.[24]

In considering circumstances in which consent might be deemed to have been withheld unreasonably, Nichols and Meston suggest that:

> "a wife who refuses consent to a sale because she does not want to move to a new home on her husband obtaining employment elsewhere would no doubt be regarded as unreasonable. It would be otherwise if the sale was simply to raise money and no alternative accommodation was offered to her."[25]

An application for such an order will be refused where a transfer of property order relative to the matrimonial home is craved by the non-applicant spouse.[26]

ORDERS TRANSFERRING TENANCY[27]

A sheriff in an action for divorce may, on granting decree or within such period as he may specify on granting decree, make an order:

(i)   transferring the tenancy of a matrimonial home to a non-entitled spouse,[28] or

(ii)   where the spouses are joint or common tenants of a

---

[24] *Ibid.*, s.7(2).

[25] *The Matrimonial Homes (Family Protection) (Scotland) Act 1981*, p. 50. Cf. *Hall, supra, Perkins* v. *Perkins*, Glasgow Sheriff Court, December 11, 1984 (unreported) (consent held to be withheld unreasonably where non-applicant spouse had not lived in the matrimonial home for two years and had own accommodation and was withholding consent because of disagreement as to how proceeds of sale should be divided) and *O'Neill* v. *O'Neill*, 1987 S.L.T. (Sh.Ct.) 26 (consent held to be withheld unreasonably where purpose of withholding not to protect occupancy rights but to attempt to force the other spouse into certain actings in exchange).

[26] *Rae* v. *Rae*, 1991 S.L.T. 454.

[27] Applications for these are not competent where the tenancy is a service tenancy, a lease of a farm, croft or similar holding, a long lease or a tenancy-at-will—1981 Act, s.13(7). Note also that "tenancy" includes subtenancy, statutory tenancy as defined in s.3 of the Rent (Scotland) Act 1971 and statutory assured tenancy as defined in s.16(1) of the Housing (Scotland) Act 1988—s 22

[28] 1981 Act, s.13(1) and (2) (as amended by the Family Law (Scotland) Act 1985, Sched. 1, para. 11).

matrimonial home, vesting the tenancy in one spouse only.[29]

In either case, the court may provide for payment by the applicant spouse to the other of such compensation as seems just and reasonable in all the circumstances of the case.[30]

The court is required in determining whether or not to grant the order to have regard to all the circumstances of the case, including the matters specified in paragraphs (*a*) to (*e*) of section 3(3) of the Act and the suitability of the applicant to become the tenant (or sole tenant, as the case may be) and his or her capacity to perform the obligations under the lease.[31] All these matters should be dealt with in detail in the pleadings.

The applicant spouse must serve a copy of the application on the landlord who must have an opportunity of being heard by the court before the order may be granted.[32]

The effect of the order is to vest the tenancy (or sole tenancy, as the case may be) in the applicant spouse without intimation to the landlord, subject to all the liabilities under the lease, other than any arrears of rent for the period before the making of the order.[33] The importance of the order lies in the fact that a spouse without a right of tenancy or incidental order entitling his or her occupation is liable to ejection once the marriage is terminated by divorce.[34]

---

[29] *Ibid.*, s.13(9) and (10).

[30] *Ibid.*, s.13(1) and (9); where the matrimonial home is a secure tenancy within the meaning of Part III of the Housing (Scotland) Act 1987, no account is to be taken, in assessing the amount of any compensation to be awarded under subs. (1) or (9) of the loss, by virtue of the transfer of the tenancy of the home, of a right to purchase the home under Part I of that Act—s.13(11).

[31] *Ibid.*, s.13(3). For an illustration of circumstances justifying the granting of an order under s.13, see *McGowan* v. *McGowan*, 1986 S.L.T. 112. For illustrations of circumstances justifying the refusing of the order, see *Wilson* v. *Wilson*, Lord Wylie, January 10, 1986, unreported, *Russell* v. *Russell*, Lord Weir, February 18, 1986, unreported and *Nicoll* v. *Nicoll*, unreported.

[32] *Ibid.*, s.13(4). Intimation of the application (which is made by a crave in the initial writ or in defences—rr. 33.48(1)(*a*) and (2)(*d*) and 33.34(1)(*c*)(iii) and (2)(*b*)(i)) requires to be made to the landlord in accordance with rr. 33.7(1)(*k*) and 33.15(2) (see Chap. 1, text accompanying nn. 21 and 23).

[33] *Ibid.*, s.13(5); these remain the non-applicant spouse's responsibility.

[34] See nn. 12 and 17 and accompanying text, *supra*.

CHAPTER 6

CHILDREN

THERE are aspects of the jurisdiction, duties and powers of the sheriff court in connection with children which are of particular importance in divorce practice.

JURISDICTION OF THE COURT

The cornerstone of the sheriff court's jurisdiction as respects children in actions of divorce is section 38C of the Sheriff Courts (Scotland) Act 1907.[1] This provides that the sheriff may make, with respect to any child of the marriage to which the action relates, such order (including an interim order) as he thinks fit relating to parental rights, and may vary or recall such order. "Parental rights" means guardianship, custody or access as the case may require, and any right or authority relating to the welfare or upbringing of a child conferred on a parent by any rule of law.[2] "Child", in relation to guardianship, custody or access, means a child under the age of 16 years.[3] "Child of the marriage" includes any child who is the child of both parties to the marriage or is the child of one party to the marriage and has been accepted[4]

---

[1] As inserted by the Court of Session Act 1988, Sched. 1, para. 2. The Scottish Law Commission in their *Report on Family Law* (Scot. Law Com. No. 135, 1992) propose the repeal of this provision and its replacement by an enactment in accordance with cl. 12 in their draft Family Law (Scotland) Bill, reproduced in App. VII.

[2] 1907 Act, s.38C(2)(*a*) and the Law Reform (Parent and Child) (Scotland) Act 1986, s.8.

[3] 1907 Act, s.38C(2)(*a*) and the 1986 Act, s.8. In relation to parental rights other than guardianship, custody or access, "child" means a child under the age of 18 years—1986 Act, s.8.

[4] Whether a child has been so accepted is a question of fact. Where the child has resided with the parties *en famille* and has been supported over a period of time by the "other party," this *prima facie* indicates acceptance of the child as one of the family: *cf. Hart* v. *Hart*, 1960 S.L.T. (Notes) 33 at p. 34. See also Clive, p. 536 and *Watson* v. *Watson*, First Division, 10 December 1993, unreported. Intimation

as a child of the family by the other party.[5] A court which refuses a decree of divorce is not by virtue of such refusal prevented from making an order regulating custody or education of, or access to, a child.[6]

The court in an action of divorce with jurisdiction to entertain an application for a custody order[7] with respect to a child is entitled to make an order declining such jurisdiction. Such an order may be made if, but for certain other provisions of the Act,[8] another court in Scotland would have jurisdiction to entertain an application for a custody order[9] or a court in another part of the United Kingdom would have jurisdiction to make a custody order or an order varying a custody order,[10] *and* the court considers that it would be more appropriate for matters relating

---

of the action must be made to any third party liable to maintain such a child (see r. 33.7(1)(*e*)(ii), set forth in Chap. 1, text accompanying n. 15). A child of which neither party is a parent or custodier is not a "child of the marriage"—*Bradley* v. *Bradley*, 1987 S.C.L.R. 62.

[5] 1907 Act, s.38C(2)(*b*).

[6] Family Law (Scotland) Act 1985, s.21. Note that jurisdiction to make such orders is also preserved by s.9(1) of the Matrimonial Proceedings (Children) Act 1958 in the event of the granting of decree of absolvitor or of dismissal at any time after proof on the merits has been allowed. This however is subject to s.13(2) of the Family Law Act 1986, which enables such orders to be made in those circumstances only where the application for the order has been made on or before such dismissal or the granting of decree of absolvitor. It is hard to figure circumstances in which a party in default against whom decree is pronounced in terms of ordinary cause rule 33.37 would also be invoking, successfully, s.9(1) of the 1958 Act. The Scottish Law Commission in their *Report on Family Law* (Scot. Law Com. No.135, 1992) propose the repeal of s.21 of the 1985 Act, so far as relevant to the above, and s.9 of the 1958 Act, and their replacement by an enactment in accordance with cl.12(2)(*b*) in their draft Family Law (Scotland) Bill, reproduced in App. VII.

[7] "Custody order" is defined by s.1(1)(*b*) of the Family Law Act 1986 as "an order made by a court of civil jurisdiction in Scotland under any enactment or rule of law with respect to the custody, care or control of a child, access to a child or the education or upbringing of a child," excepting *inter alia* (a) an order committing the care of a child to, or placing the child under the supervision of, a local authority; (b) an order for the delivery of a child or other order for the enforcement of a custody order; and (c) (subject to ss.32 and 40 of the Act) an order made before the date of the commencement of Pt. 1 of the Act or on an application made before that date—s.1(1)(*b*) and (3)(*a*) and (*b*). A "child" is a person who has not attained the age of 16 years—s.18(1).

[8] *Viz.* ss.3(2), 6(3), 11(1), 20(2) and 23(3) (jurisdiction excluded where matrimonial proceedings in respect of the child's parents' marriage continuing elsewhere in the U.K.).

[9] s.13(6)(*a*)(i).

[10] s.13(6)(*a*)(ii).

to the custody of that child to be determined in that other court or part.[11] The court may recall such an order declining jurisdiction.[12] An application for a custody order may be refused in any case where the matter in question has already been determined in other proceedings.[13]

DUTIES OF THE COURT

A. The court is bound not to grant decree of divorce unless and until satisfied as respects every child for whose custody it has power to make provision in that action—

(a) that arrangements have been made for the care and upbringing of the child and that those arrangements are satisfactory or are the best which can be devised in the circumstances; or

(b) that it is impracticable for the party or parties appearing before the court to make any such arrangements.[14]

The foregoing does not apply where the court has made an order declining jurisdiction or sisting the proceedings in respect of an application for a custody order relative to the child,[15] nor where it appears to the court that there are circumstances making it desirable that decree should be granted without delay and the court has obtained a satisfactory undertaking from either or both parties to bring the question of the arrangements for the children before the court within a specified time.[16]

The court has power, for the purpose of satisfying itself as to the proposed arrangements for the care and upbringing of any child as to whose custody the court has power to make orders, to appoint an appropriate local authority to investigate and report to

---

[11] s.13(6)(*b*). Alternatively, if it appears to the court that proceedings are likely to be taken in the other, more appropriate, court, it may at any stage sist the proceedings on the application before it—s.14(2)(*b*). The court may do likewise, irrespective of appropriateness, if it appears to it that proceedings with respect to which the application relates are continuing outside Scotland or in another court in Scotland—s.13(2)(*a*).

[12] *Ibid.*, s.13(7).

[13] *Ibid.*, s.14(1).

[14] 1958 Act, s.8(1), as amended by the Law Reform (Parent and Child) (Scotland) Act 1986, Sched. 2 and the Family Law Act 1986, Sched. 1, para 4. As to proposals to repeal this section, see n. 17 *infra*.

[15] *Ibid.*

[16] 1958 Act, s.8 (2).

the court on all the circumstances of the child and on the proposed arrangements for the care and upbringing of the child.[17] If on consideration of the report the court, either *ex proprio motu* or on the application of any person concerned, thinks it expedient to do so, it may require the person who furnished the report to appear and to be examined on oath regarding any matter dealt with in the report, and such person may be examined or cross-examined accordingly.[18]

Subject to the foregoing, evidence falls to be presented in affidavit form in accordance with rule 33.28 (3).[19]

B. As in any other proceedings in which parental rights are in question, the court in actions of divorce must regard the welfare of the child involved as the paramount consideration and must not make any order relating to parental rights unless it is satisfied that to do so will be in the interests of the child.[20]

Where the application for the order is being considered after proof, the court requires to be so satisfied on balance of probabilities.[21] When the sheriff is dealing with a motion for an interim order, what he requires to do is to consider all the material information placed before him, and then decide whether he is satisfied that it would be in the interests of the child to make the order.[22]

---

[17] *Ibid.*, s.11 (1), the power being stated to be without prejudice to the power of the court to appoint any other person, not being an officer of the local authority. The power should only be exercised where every reasonable method of obtaining evidence has been attempted unsuccessfully (*Wallace* v. *Wallace*, 1963 S.C. 256 at p. 258). *Quaere* whether, reading s.11 (1) with s.8 (1)(*a*), the power is exerciseable so as to appoint a local authority to investigate and report with regard to an application for interim custody or interim access, as r. 33.21(1)(*a*) ("at any stage of a family action") implies. The Scottish Law Commission in their *Report on Family Law* (Scot. Law Com. No. 135, 1992) propose amendment of the power set forth in s.11(1) so as to make it exerciseable not only for the purpose of the court's satisfying itself as to the proposed arrangements for the child's care and upbringing but also "where the court is considering any question relating to the care and upbringing of a child." They further propose the replacement of s.8 of the 1958 Act (see text accompanying n. 14 *supra*) by an enactment in accordance with cl. 14 (1) and (2) of their draft Family Law (Scotland) Bill, reproduced in App. VII.

[18] 1958 Act, s.11 (4).

[19] See Chap. 1, text accompanying n. 32. The applicable Practice Note or Act of Court should be consulted (see App. III).

[20] Law Reform (Parent and Child) (Scotland) Act 1986, s.3(2). *Cf.* cl. 12 (3) of the draft Family Law (Scotland) Bill, reproduced in App. VII.

[21] *F* v. *F*, 1991 S.L.T. 357 at p. 362G.

[22] *Armstrong* v. *Gibson*, 1991 S.L.T. 193 at p. 194L.

POWERS OF THE COURT

The court's powers in connection with children in divorce actions are wide and include[23] (in addition to certain restricted powers to make provision for the maintenance of children, not discussed in detail herein[24]) powers to make orders for or in respect of custody

---

[23] See Chap. 4 as to the power of the court to prevent the removal of children. Note that the court has a statutory power in relation to court proceedings to restrict publicity concerning a person under the age of 17 years (see *C*. v. *S*., 1989 S.L.T. 168).

[24] The court's powers to make provision for the maintenance of children have been very largely curtailed by the Child Support Act 1991. Aside from transitional arrangements (*infra*), the residual role of the courts in this respect, prescribed by s.8 of the Act is, broadly, confined to: (a) revoking maintenance orders (subs.(3)); (b) making maintenance orders giving effect to written agreements (subs.(5)); (c) making top up maintenance orders (subs.(6)); (d) making maintenance orders requiring payees to meet some or all of the expenses incurred in connection with the provision of instruction at an educational establishment or training for a trade, profession or vocation (subs.(7)); (e) making certain maintenance orders in relation to disabled children (subs. (8) and (9)); and (f) making maintenance orders against a person with care of the child (subs.(10)). See, generally, Clive, pp. 556–563 and article (1993)38 J.L.S.474. Applications for aliment require to be made by a crave in the initial writ or defences, as the case may be or, where the applicant is a third party, by minute (r. 33.39 (1) and (2)(*b*)), unless made after decree (in which case the application is made by minute in the original process—r. 33.45(1)). Applications for interim aliment in either case are made by motion (rr. 33.43(*a*)(i) and 33.45(2)). An application may be made by a person over 18 years for aliment or interim aliment in terms of r. 33.46. The arrangements for the transition from the pre-existing court based system to that operated by the Child Support Agency are described in Part Four of the DSS Guidance Notes *inter alia* as follows:

"The effectiveness of the Agency would be impaired if its final full operational capacity were attempted from the outset and so it will not be fully operational until [April] 1997, the majority of cases being taken on by 1996. Cases will be taken on according to the following phased timetable, which will ensure the smooth transition from the court-based system:

From April 1993, any new case, whether Income Support, Family Credit or Disability Working Allowance is in payment or not, will be taken on by the Agency. From April 1993 to April 1996, existing Income Support, Family Credit or Disability Working Allowance cases will be taken on. Priority will be given to those cases where a change of circumstances occurs which affects maintenance. On current assumptions, the Child Support Agency will start from April 1996 to take on cases where there is an existing maintenance arrangement (either a voluntary agreement, a maintenance agreement or a court order) and none of the relevant benefits listed above is in payment. Cases will be taken on gradually according to the surname of the person with care as follows:

and access[25] and, in exceptional circumstances, certain orders under the Matrimonial Proceedings (Children) Act 1958 regarding the care and supervision of children.

Custody and access orders

Section 38C of the Sheriff Courts (Scotland) Act 1907 confers upon the court "the widest and most general discretion"[26] in

April 1996	–	A – D
July 1996	–	E – K
October 1996	–	L – R
January 1997	–	S – Z

During the period from April 1993 to April 1996 the courts will retain all of their powers to vary an order. From April 1996, once the Agency has acquired jurisdiction to deal with a particular case, the courts will no longer have the power to make or vary an order in that case. Where the parties decide that they do not want an assessment from the Agency and wish to retain their order, they will be able to do so, although they will not be able to go to court to get the order varied. The courts will retain the power to make consent orders from written agreements so long as the terms of the order are, in all material respects, the same as the agreement."

The court's powers to vary an order after decree during the transitional period are exerciseable upon a material change of circumstances (Family Law (Scotland) Act 1985, s.5(1)) and may be sought to be invoked by way of minute lodged in the original process (r. 33.45(1)). Where such a minute has been lodged, any party may lodge a motion for an interim order which may be made pending the determination of the application (r. 33.45(2)). The court has power to backdate a variation, in terms of s.5(2) of the 1985 Act, to the date of the application for variation or, on special cause shown, to a date prior to that (the last being a power to be exercised sparingly—*Hannah* v. *Hannah*, 1988 S.L.T. 82 and *Dalgleish* v. *Robinson*, 1991 S.C.L.R. 892), and in that event to order any sums paid under the decree to be repaid (1985 Act, s.5(4)). (As to variation of an order for interim aliment in a depending action, see Chap. 7, text accompanying nn. 9 to 11 and r. 33.43(*a*)(i)). In any action in which an order for aliment is sought, or is sought to be varied or recalled, the pleadings of the applicant must include an averment stating whether and, if so, when and by whom, a maintenance order has been granted in favour of or against that party or of any other person in respect of whom the order is sought (r. 33.5). See also r. 33.6(2) with respect to applications for top up maintenance orders; r. 33.6(3) in relation to applications not covered by the Child Support Act 1991; and r. 33.6(5) with regard to actions involving parties in respect of whom a decision has been made in any application, review or appeal under the 1991 Act relating to any child of those parties.

[25] Other parental rights (see text accompanying n. 2 *supra*) are not discussed within these pages. The Scottish Law Commission in their *Report on Family Law* (Scot. Law Com. No. 135, 1992) propose the replacement of orders for custody and access with those set forth in cl. 12(1) of their draft Family Law (Scotland) Bill, reproduced in App. VII.

[26] *Per* the Lord Chancellor in *Symington* v. *Symington* (1875) 2 R.(H.L.) 41 at p. 43, under reference to the provision's precursor.

relation to custody and access. An appellate court could only interfere with any decision taken in exercise of this discretion if it were to be satisfied that the judge of first instance had exercised his discretion upon a wrong principle or that, his decision being so plainly wrong, he must have exercised his discretion wrongly.[27]

In the fulfilment of its duty to regard the welfare of the child as the paramount consideration, and in the exercise of its aforesaid discretion, the court may make an award or interim award[28] of custody[29] or access[30] in favour of any party to the action (including a third party[31]). Joint custody is competent but rarely appropriate.[32] Where custody or access is in dispute, the sheriff may, at any stage in the proceedings, where he considers it appropriate to do so, refer that dispute to a specified family mediation and conciliation service.[33] Where the sheriff of his own

---

[27] *Per* Lord President Emslie in *Britton* v. *Central Regional Council*, 1986 S.L.T. 207 at p. 208.

[28] An award of interim custody of unlimited duration made without intimation of the application to the non-applicant spouse is of questionable competency and in any event inappropriate where there is no question of the non-applicant spouse leaving the country and no averment of imminent danger to the child (*Nelson* v. *Nelson*, 1989 S.L.T. (Sh.Ct.) 18 and *Anderson* v. *Anderson*, 1992 S.C.L.R. 764). An award of interim access may not competently be appealed without leave of the sheriff (*Black* v. *Black*, 1991 S.L.T. (Sh.Ct.) 5). Application for interim custody of, or interim access to, a child requires to be made by motion—r. 33.43(*a*)(ii).

[29] It will seldom be appropriate to award custody in favour of a person who cannot exercise the right for the time being (*e.g.* where child is subject to supervision requirement)—F. v. F., 1991 S.L.T. 357 at p. 363 I.

[30] The competency of awarding access without awarding custody was affirmed in *Huddart* v. *Huddart*, 1960 S.C. 300; 1960 S.L.T. 275. Access was awarded to one parent and an award of custody refused to the other in *Potter* v. *Potter*, 1993 S.L.T. (Sh.Ct.) 51.

[31] Section 3(1) of the Law Reform (Parent and Child) (Scotland) Act 1986 entitles any person claiming interest to apply to the court for an order relating to parental rights. Such person need not be a parent or a person claiming to be a parent—F. v. F., *supra*. Such application is subject to s.3(2) of the 1986 Act (text accompanying n. 20 *supra*). Any such third party applicant is subject to the provisions of the Children Act 1975, ss.47 to 49 (as to which, see Clive, pp. 523 and 524), and rr. 33.7(1)(*e*) to (*h*) and (4) and 33.15 (2) (intimation), 33.12 (execution of service on, or intimation to, local authority) and 33.19 (consents to grant of custody). See Chap. 1, n. 17 and accompanying text.

[32] "The idea of joint custody raises many practical problems, and I should have thought that the occasions when it is in the child's best interests must be rare" (*per* Sheriff Principal Sir Frederick O'Brien in *McKechnie* v. *McKechnie*, 1990 S.L.T. (Sh.Ct.) 75 at p. 76).

[33] r. 33.22.

motion or on the motion of a party is considering making an award of access or interim access subject to supervision by the social work department of a local authority, he requires to ordain the party moving for access or interim access to intimate to the chief executive of that local authority (where not already a party to the action and represented at the hearing at which the issue arises)—(a) the terms of any relevant motion; (b) the intention of the sheriff to order that access be supervised by the social work department; and (c) that the local authority shall, within such period as the sheriff has determined—(i) notify the sheriff clerk whether it intends to make representations to the sheriff; and (ii) where it intends to make representations in writing, to do so within that period.[34] Applications for the court to exercise its powers to award custody or access in her favour[35] may be made by the pursuer by inserting a crave therefor in the initial writ; by the defender by inserting a crave in defences[36]; and by a third party by way of a minute.[37]

Ordinary cause rule 33.9(*b*) provides that unless the sheriff on cause shown otherwise directs, a warrant for citation shall not be granted in an action where he may make an order in respect of the custody of a child without there being produced with the initial writ an extract of the relevant entry in the register of births or equivalent document.

Rule 33.3(1)(*a*) requires that a party who makes an application for a custody order shall make averments in his pleadings giving particulars of any other proceedings known to him (whether in Scotland or elsewhere and whether concluded or not) which relate to the child in respect of whom the custody order is sought.[38] Where such other proceedings are continuing or have taken place and the averments of the applicant for such a custody order (a) do not contain particulars of the other proceedings, or (b) contain particulars which are incomplete or incorrect, any defences or minute (as the case may be) lodged by any person must include such particulars or such further or correct particulars as are known to him.[39]

Where a child in respect of whom the sheriff may make an order

---

[34] r. 33.25.
[35] A crave that another party be awarded custody or access is incompetent (*T* v. *T*, 1987 S.L.T. (Sh.Ct.) 74).
[36] r. 33.39(1)(*a*) and (2)(*a*).
[37] r. 33.39(1)(*b*) and (2)(*a*).
[38] The duty to give such particulars is statutory: Family Law Act 1986, s.39.
[39] r. 33.3(2).

for any parental rights is in the care of a local authority, or is a child who, being a child of one party to the marriage, has been accepted as a child of the family by the other party to the marriage and who is liable to be maintained by a third party or is a child in respect of whom a third party exercises parental rights *de facto*, intimation falls to be made in terms of rules 33.7(1)(*e*) and 33.15 (2).[40] Intimation requires also to be given to any parent or guardian of the child who is not a party to the action[41]; and "in an action which affects a child" to that child if not a party to the action.[42] In an action where the pursuer craves the custody of a child and she is (i) not a parent of that child, and (ii) resident in Scotland when the initial writ is lodged, she must include a crave for a warrant for intimation to the local authority within which area the pursuer resides[43]; and where the pursuer (a) craves the custody of a child, and (b) is not resident in Scotland when the initial writ is lodged for warranting, she must include a crave for an order for intimation to such local authority as the sheriff thinks fit.[44]

In order to exercise its powers, the court is entitled to require to be fully informed and at the interim stage may appoint a reporter to investigate and report to the court on the circumstances of a child.[45] On making such appointment, the sheriff requires to direct that the party who sought the appointment or, where the court makes the appointment of its own motion, the pursuer or minuter (as the case may be) shall (a) instruct the reporter, and (b) be responsible, in the first instance, for the fees and outlays of the reporter appointed.[46] The party who sought the appointment or, where the sheriff makes the appointment of his own motion, the pursuer or minuter (as the case may be) is required, within 7 days after the date of the appointment, to intimate the name and address of the reporter to any local authority to which intimation

---

[40] See Chap. 1, text accompanying nn. 15 and 23.

[41] rr. 33.7(1)(*f*) and 33.15(2) (see Chap. 1, text accompanying nn. 16 and 23).

[42] rr. 33.7(1)(*h*) and 33.15(2) (see Chap. 1, n. 18 and text accompanying that footnote and n. 23).

[43] rr. 33.7(1)(*g*) and 33.15(2) (see Chap. 1, text accompanying nn. 17 and 23). A notice of intimation in Form F8 must be attached to the initial writ intimated to that authority.

[44] rr. 33.7(4) and 33.15(2) (see Chap. 1, n. 17 and text accompanying n. 23). Intimation is in Form F8.

[45] Such reporter may be an advocate or a solicitor. *Quaere* whether there is a statutory power to appoint a local authority at the interim stage see n. 17 *supra*. Note that a report is not evidence—*Whitecross* v. *Whitecross*, 1977 S.L.T. 255.

[46] r. 33.21(2).

of the action has been made.[47] On completion of his report, the reporter is required to send it, with a copy of it for each party, to the sheriff clerk who must upon receipt send a copy to each party.[48] Where a reporter has been appointed, an application for the custody of the child concerned cannot be determined until the report has been lodged.[49]

When considering an application for custody or interim custody, the court will have regard to a variety of matters. A primary concern is the physical welfare of the child (*i.e.* matters of health, cleanliness, diet, accommodation, clothing, etc.). The parties' respective fitness to cater for such physical needs of the child will be compared. The capacity of each party to provide for the happiness and psychological welfare of the child will also be examined. The ability to give the child emotional security over the long term is of great importance, whereas mere ability to make better provision for the material welfare of the child is not normally significant. The parties' respective characters and circumstances and the relationship between each of them and the child will be assessed. The scope of the inquiry may be widened to take account of other people, including siblings and relatives, and the wishes of the child. Factors such as the age of the child, the parties' past conduct so far as relevant to the child's welfare and the extent to which it might disadvantage the child to disturb the *status quo* may be important considerations, as may many other factors, both short and long term.[50]

In access questions the criteria that are applicable are inevitably narrower: a parent, for example, who is incapable of looking after a child may nonetheless serve that child's best interests by being allowed access to him or her. The court will be concerned to weigh the benefits and disadvantages for the child of maintaining or resuming contact with the applicant (and, perhaps, his side of the family) and to assess the many factors that may be relevant thereto, such as, for example: the extent of past contact between the applicant and the child; the likely effect on the child in the short and in the longer term of allowing or disallowing access; the

---

[47] r. 33.21(3).
[48] r. 33.21(4) and (5).
[49] r. 33.21(6).
[50] See, generally, Clive at pp. 540–546 and cases cited therein.

likely effect of allowing supervised access; and the wishes[51] of the child.[52]

Section 33(1) of the Family Law Act 1986 entitles the court, where in proceedings for or relating to a custody order in respect of a child there is not available to it adequate information as to where the child is, to order any person who it has reason to believe may have relevant information to disclose it to the court. Application for the order requires to be made by motion; and the sheriff may ordain the person against whom the order has been made to appear before him or to lodge an affidavit.[53] A person cannot be excused from complying with such an order by reason that to do so may incriminate him or his spouse of an offence; but a statement or admission made in compliance with the order is not admissible in evidence against either of them in proceedings for any offence other than perjury.[54]

The sheriff has power at common law where an order for custody or access is sought to be enforced (i) to appoint a commissioner to take evidence on oath from such persons as there are reasonable grounds to believe may have information which would enable officers of the court to find the child concerned[55]; and (ii) to grant warrant to sheriff officers to search for and take possession of the child.[56]

Where (and only where) the sheriff has jurisdiction to make a custody order, he may entertain an application for an order, otherwise than to implement a custody order, for the delivery of a child by one parent to the other or by one party to a marriage to the other.[57] The foregoing is without prejudice to the sheriff's jurisdiction to entertain an application by a parent who is entitled

---

[51] The sheriff may with the parties' consent interview the child in order to ascertain its wishes, but no such interview can be substituted for the recognised procedure (with its inbuilt rules and safeguards) of having issues of custody and access determined by proof in open court (*Macdonald* v. *Macdonald*, 1985 S.L.T. 244). The value of any interview may depend on the age of the child (*Gover* v. *Gover*, 1969 S.L.T. (Notes) 78). *Cf.* cl. 12(5) in App. VII.

[52] See, generally, Clive at pp. 547–548 and cases cited therein.

[53] r. 33.23.

[54] 1986 Act, s.33(2).

[55] *Abusaif* v. *Abusaif*, 1984 S.L.T. 90.

[56] *Caldwell* v. *Caldwell*, 1983 S.L.T. 610.

[57] s.17(1) and (3). The latter application would concern a child of one of the parties to the marriage accepted as one of the family by the other.

to the custody of a child for an order for the delivery of the child
from a parent who is not so entitled.[58]

Where breach of an interim order relating to access is alleged,
the court may ordain the custodier to appear at the bar to answer
the allegation; and where such breach is denied, minute and
answers (or a report) may be ordered.[59] Where breach of a final
order is alleged, procedure is by ordinary action commenced by
initial writ.[60] If the court is satisfied that the order or interim order
has been breached, the custodier may be fined, imprisoned or
simply admonished as to his or her duties as custodier:

> "The responsibility for making access arrangements work rests to a
> substantial extent upon the [custodier] and ... this involves not only
> encouraging the children to see [the party entitled to access] but also
> trying to create a climate of opinion in which they view [him or her]
> in a reasonable and well-disposed light."[61]

The parties may agree questions of custody and access by joint
minute or otherwise but no such agreement can bind the court.[62]
The sheriff may grant decree in respect of those parts of the joint
minute in relation to which he could otherwise make an order,
whether or not such a decree would include a matter for which
there was no crave.[63]

A custody order ceases to have effect once the child reaches the
age of 16 years. Where (a) a custody order, or an order varying a
custody order, competently made by another court in any part of
the United Kingdom with respect to a child, or (b) an order for the
custody of a child which is made outside the United Kingdom and
recognised by virtue of the 1986 Act, comes into force, a custody
order relating to that child already made by a court in Scotland
ceases to have effect so far as it makes provision for any matter for
which the same or different provision is made by the order of the
other court in the United Kingdom or, as the case may be, the

---

[58] s.17(2). The court has power at common law to give effect to any order by it for
custody or access by granting an order for delivery, failure to comply with
which is punishable as a contempt of court (*Brown* v. *Brown*, 1948 S.C. 5 and
Thomson v. *Thomson*, 1979 S.L.T. (Sh.Ct.) 11).

[59] Macphail, *Sheriff Court Practice*, para. 22–152; and *Celso* v. *Celso*, 1992 S.C.L.R.
175.

[60] *Celso, cit. supra.*

[61] *Per* Lord Jauncey in *Cosh* v. *Cosh*, 1979 S.L.T. (Notes) 72 at p. 73; see also *Blance* v.
Blance, 1978 S.L.T. 74 and *Brannigan* v. *Brannigan*, 1979 S.L.T. (Notes) 73.

[62] *Robson* v. *Robson*, 1973 S.L.T. (Notes) 4; *Anderson* v. *Anderson*, 1989 S.C.L.R. 475;
McKechnie v. *McKechnie*, 1990 S.L.T. (Sh.Ct.) 75.

[63] r. 33.26.

order so recognised.[64] Where a custody order made by a court in Scotland thus ceases to have effect so far as it makes provision for any matter, that court has no power to vary it so as to make provision for that matter.[65] Otherwise, the court may vary,[66] or recall, any custody order made by it notwithstanding that it would no longer have jurisdiction to make the original order.[67]

Application after final decree for, or for the variation or recall of, an order relating to parental rights, requires to be made by minute in the process of the action to which the application relates.[68] Where a minute has been lodged, any party may apply by motion for any interim order which may be made pending the determination of the application.[69]

Care and supervision orders[70]

Where it appears to the court that there are exceptional circumstances making it impracticable or undesirable for the child to be entrusted to either of the parties to the marriage, the court may, if it thinks fit, make an order committing the care of the child to any other individual or to a local authority.[71]

Where the sheriff is considering making such an order, he must ordain one of the parties to intimate to that person or to the chief

---

[64] 1986 Act, ss.15(1) and 26. Any order made under s.12(1) of the 1958 Act for supervision of a child by a local authority ceases to have effect where any person who is entitled to the custody of the child ceases to be so entitled by virtue of s.15 (1)—s.15(4).

[65] *Ibid.*, s.15(2).

[66] An order varying an original order means any custody order made with respect to the same child as the original order was made—s.13(3).

[67] s.15(2), subject to ss.11(1) and 13(4) of the Act.

[68] r. 33.44(1)(*a*).

[69] r. 33.44(2).

[70] The phrase is employed here to denote orders under sections 10 and 12, respectively, of the Matrimonial Proceedings (Children) Act 1958. The Scottish Law Commission in their *Report on Family Law* (Scot. Law Com. No. 135, 1992) propose the repeal of these provisions and their replacement by an amendment to the Social Work (Scotland) Act 1968 as set forth in cl. 15 of their draft Family Law (Scotland) Bill, reproduced in App. VII.

[71] 1958 Act, s.10(1). Where the court commits the care of the child to a local authority the authority specified in the order shall be the council of the region or islands area in which the child was, in the opinion of the court, resident before the order was made—s.10(2). Where such an order is made, the sheriff clerk must send a copy of the interlocutor making the order and a notice of intimation in Form F29 to the chief executive of the local authority or other person concerned—r. 33.41.

executive of the appropriate local authority (as the case may be) where not already a party to the action and represented at the hearing at which the issue arises (a) a copy of the pleadings (including any adjustments and amendments); (b) the terms of any relevant motion; and (c) notice of intimation in Form F28 requiring any representations which that person or that local authority wishes to make to the sheriff to be made by minute in the process of the action within the period specified.[72]

While the order remains in force any motion or minute lodged which relates to the child must be intimated to the chief executive of the local authority or other person concerned.[73] For so long as the care of a child is committed to a local authority, that child shall continue in that care notwithstanding any claim by a parent or other person.[74] It is the duty of any parent or guardian of a child committed to the care of a local authority to secure that the authority are informed of his address for the time being.[75]

Where it appears to the court that there are exceptional circumstances making it desirable that a child should be under the supervision of an independent person, the court may, as respects any period during which the child is committed to the custody of any person, make an order placing the child under the supervision of a local authority.[76] The sheriff is obliged first to ordain intimation as with respect to care orders.[77]

Such an order cannot be made in respect of a child who is subject to an order committing him or her to the care of a local authority.[78] Where such an order has been made, any motion or minute lodged which relates to the child must be intimated to the chief executive of the local authority.[73] Such an order having been made, the local authority in question has no locus to become a party minuter in order to crave the variation or recall of an award of custody or access.[79]

---

[72] r. 33.40. The sheriff's duty to hear representations from the local authority (including any as to the making of an order for payments for the maintenance and education of the child) is statutory—1958 Act, s.10(2).

[73] r. 33.42.

[74] *Ibid.*, s.10(3).

[75] *Ibid.*, s.10(6).

[76] *Ibid.*, s.12(1). Where such an order is made, the sheriff clerk must send a copy of the interlocutor making the order and a notice of intimation in Form F29 to the chief executive of the local authority—r. 33.41.

[77] r. 33.40—see text accompanying n. 72 *supra.*

[78] *Ibid.*, s.12(4).

[73] r. 33.42.

[79] *Black* v. *Black*, 1988 S.L.T. (Sh.Ct.) 24.

An order made during the course of the proceedings ceases to have effect when the action ceases to be pending.[80] An application to the sheriff after decree for, or for the variation or recall of, a care or supervision order requires to be made by minute in the original process.[81] Where a minute is lodged, any party may apply by motion for an interim order pending the determination of the application.[82]

---

[80] *Hunt* v. *Hunt*, 1987 S.L.T. 672. See also n. 64 *supra*.
[81] r. 33.44(1)(*b*) and (*c*). Application for such variation or recall *pendente lite* requires to be made by motion—r. 33.43(*b*).
[82] r. 33.44(2).

CHAPTER 7

MONEY

THE subject of money in the context of divorce (excepting maintenance for children) is discussed in this chapter; and the court's powers to make orders relative to the subject under the Family Law (Scotland) Act 1985[1] before, upon, or after the granting of divorce are examined.

---

[1] In actions brought before September 1, 1986 (the date of commencement of the Family Law (Scotland) Act 1985) s.5 of the Divorce (Scotland) Act 1976 continues to operate—1985 Act, s.28(3). In the continued operation of s.5, the court's power under subs. (4) to vary an order for payment of periodical allowance now includes power to make such an order for a definite or an indefinite period or until the happening of a specified event—1985 Act, s.28(3) (*b*). The court cannot exercise such additional power unless and until a change of circumstances justifying variation in terms of s.5(4) has been demonstrated— *Wilson* v. *Wilson*, 1987 S.L.T. 721, *Collins* v. *Collins*, 1989 S.L.T. 194 and *McPherson* v. *McPherson*, 1989 S.L.T. 231. (Note (i) that the passing of the 1985 Act is not in itself a relevant change of circumstances—*Grindlay* v. *Grindlay*, 1987 S.L.T. 264 and *Caven* v. *Caven*, 1987 S.L.T. 761; and (ii) that the factors relevant to the exercise of such additional power under s.28(3) are not necessarily the same as those which are relevant to a consideration of the amount of the periodical allowance for the time being—*Nimmo* v. *Nimmo*, 1989 G.W.D. 30–1810.) The court also has no such additional power under s.28(3) in respect of an application for an award of a periodical allowance under s.5(3) of the 1976 Act (*viz.* where an application is made after decree of divorce, no such award having previously been made)—*Grindlay*, *cit. supra*, and *Ross* v. *Ross*, 1988 S.C.L.R. 267. The power of the court to vary or recall an order under s.5(4) does not include power to backdate such variation or recall (*Walker* v. *Walker*, 1991 S.C.L.R. 419; *Wilson* v. *Wilson*, 1992 S.L.T. 664 and cases cited therein), which additional power the Scottish Law Commission in their *Report on Family Law* (Scot. Law Com. No. 135, 1992) propose should be bestowed by amendment to s.28(3) of the 1985 Act. The court does have power to vary a provision in an earlier order restricting the period during which periodical allowance will be payable— *McPherson*, *cit. supra*, (Note also in *McPherson* the observation that if a sheriff wishes to award periodical allowance for a definite period all he requires to do is to find the applicant entitled to the periodical allowance up to a specified date). The court has no duty, when considering applications in pre-1985 Act divorce actions, to have regard to the terms of ss.9 and 11 of the 1985 Act—*Wilson*, *cit. supra*, and *Collins*, *cit. supra*. In any such application, the court's only task, if a change of circumstances has been demonstrated, is to decide whether, in all the circumstances of the case, a variation ought properly to be made—*Collins*, *cit.*

ORDERS MADE BEFORE THE GRANTING OF DECREE

Interim aliment orders

Either party to an action of divorce may claim interim aliment.[2] Whether or not the claim is disputed, the court may award the sum claimed or any lesser sum or may refuse to make an award.[3] An award of interim aliment must consist of an award of periodical payments payable only until the date of the disposal of the action or such earlier date as the court may specify.[4]

The court may order either party to provide details of his resources,[5] and may reasonably expect the parties to produce documentary evidence of their respective net[6] incomes at any hearing on a claim for interim aliment. In deciding what award of interim aliment if any to make, the court may have regard to considerations applicable in determining the amount to award in respect of a claim for aliment, namely needs, earning capacity and general circumstances.[7]

Awards of interim aliment are within the discretion of the sheriff and an appellate court could only interfere with any decision taken in exercise of this discretion if it were to be satisfied that the judge of first instance had erred in law, or that he had failed to notice a relevant factor, or that

---

supra. For illustration, see *Jenkins* v. *Jenkins*, 1991 S.L.T. 373, *Kerray* v. *Kerray*, 1991 S.L.T. 613 and *Mitchell* v. *Mitchell*, 1993 S.L.T. 419.

[2] s.6(1)(*b*). Application must be made by motion—r. 33.50.

[3] s.6(2).

[4] s.6(3).

[5] s.20, considered *infra.* "Resources" means present and foreseeable resources— s.27(1).

[6] As in *Wiseman* v. *Wiseman*, 1989 S.C.L.R. 757 and *Pryde* v. *Pryde*, 1991 S.L.T. (Sh.Ct.) 26. But see *MacInnes* v. *MacInnes*, 1993 S.L.T. 1108.

[7] *McGeachie* v. *McGeachie*, 1989 S.C.L.R. 99 ("While it is true that the criteria set out in s.4 of the 1985 Act do not by virtue of the Act apply to interim aliment awards ... these criteria are consistent with pre-existing law and practice in relation to the determination of interim aliment. .... [N] eeds, earning capacity and general circumstances are all proper elements to consider when awarding interim aliment." (*per* Sheriff Principal Caplan at p. 100)). *Quaere* whether, and if so when, a spouse could reasonably expect to be alimented when cohabiting with a third party (*cf. Brunton* v. *Brunton*, 1986 S.L.T. 49 and *Kavanagh* v. *Kavanagh*, 1989 S.L.T. 134). See also *Munro* v. *Munro*, 1986 S.L.T. 72 and *Henderson* v. *Henderson*, 1991 G.W.D. 31–1864 (relevance of paying spouse's cohabitant's earnings).

he had arrived at a wholly unreasonable decision.[8]

An award of interim aliment may be varied or recalled by an order of the court[9] but no such variation or recall can be backdated.[10] It has been held that variation of an award of interim aliment is competent without a change of circumstances having been established, there requiring only to be a sufficient reason to justify a variation.[11]

Incidental orders

An incidental order may be made under section 8(2) of the Act before, as well as on or after, the granting or refusal of decree of divorce.[12] The orders which fall within the definition of an incidental order and the considerations applicable to the making thereof are detailed *infra*. An incidental order may be varied or recalled by subsequent order on cause shown.[13]

Orders for provision of details of resources

By virtue of section 20 of the Act, the court may order either party to provide details of his resources.[14] The power may be exercised even where there is no suggestion that the party called upon to provide details is in some way concealing some resource.[15] If the party so called upon fails to provide details of his present and foreseeable resources he will be in contempt of an

---

[8] *Begg* v. *Begg*, 1987 S.C.L.R. 704 at p. 705. An appeal without leave of the sheriff against an award of interim aliment or the refusal of an application for interim aliment is incompetent (*Rixson* v. *Rixson*, 1990 S.L.T. (Sh.Ct.) 5, *Hulme* v. *Hulme*, 1990 S.L.T. (Sh.Ct.) 25, *Dickson* v. *Dickson*, 1990 S.L.T. (Sh.Ct.) 80 and *Richardson* v. *Richardson*, 1991 S.L.T. (Sh.Ct.) 7).

[9] 1985 Act, s.6(4). The provisions of s.6 apply to an award so varied and the claim therefor as they applied to the original award and the claim therefor—*ibid.* Application for variation or recall must be made by motion—r. 33.50.

[10] *McColl* v. *McColl*, 1993 S.L.T. 617.

[11] *Bisset* v. *Bisset*, 1993 S.C.L.R. 284.

[12] *Ibid.*, s.14(1), excepting the orders specified in the text accompanying nn. 8 and 9 *infra*. For illustrations of circumstances in which incidental orders sought *pendente lite* were refused as premature, see *McKeown* v. *McKeown*, 1988 S.C.L.R. 355 and *Demarco* v. *Demarco*, 1990 S.C.L.R. 635. Application may be made by motion, except that the sheriff is not bound to determine such a motion if he considers that the application should properly be by a crave in the initial writ or defences, as the case may be—r. 33.49(1).

[13] s.14(4). Application in a depending action for such variation or recall must be made by minute in the process of the action to which the application relates—r. 33.49(2).

[14] "Resources" means present and foreseeable resources—s.27(1).

[15] *Lawrence* v. *Lawrence*, 1992 S.C.L.R. 199.

order of court.[16] Section 20 does not however give the court power to conduct an inquiry as to the extent of the disclosure.[17] In order to fulfil his obligation, the party ordered must provide a figure for the value of each item of property but does not require to produce documentation vouching the figure.[18] The sheriff is entitled to seek clarification of matters in any list of resources and may appoint the solicitor for the party concerned to appear personally before him.[19] It remains for the party claiming a specific financial provision to formulate and prove the entitlement.[20]

The power is additional to the power of the court to grant commission and diligence *inter alia* for the recovery of documents relative to a party's financial position.[21]

ORDERS MADE UPON THE GRANTING OF DECREE

In terms of section 8(1) of the Act[22]:

> "In an action for divorce, either party to the marriage may apply to the court for one or more of the following orders—
>
> (*a*)   an order for the payment of a capital sum to him by the other party to the marriage;
>
> (*aa*)   an order for the transfer of property to him by the other party to the marriage[23];

---

[16] *Nelson* v. *Nelson*, 1993 S.C.L.R. 149.

[17] *Ibid.*

[18] *Ibid.*

[19] *Ibid.*

[20] *Williamson* v. *Williamson*, 1989 S.L.T. 866 at p. 867. Once documents have been submitted in terms of s.20, however, the matter is properly before the court— *MacQueen* v. *MacQueen*, 1992 G.W.D. 28–1653.

[21] Administration of Justice (Scotland) Act 1972, s.1(1). As to expenses relative to the specification procedure, see *George* v. *George*, 1991 S.L.T. (Sh.Ct.) 8.

[22] As amended by the Law Reform (Miscellaneous Provisions) (Scotland) Act 1990, Sched. 7, para. 32.

[23] A transfer of property order subject to a balancing payment was made in *Wallis* v. *Wallis*, 1993 S.L.T. 1348. Note that in *Muir* v. *Muir*, 1993 G.W.D. 39–2593 a transfer of property order was made to the applicant spouse without her requiring to make a balancing payment (notwithstanding that such a payment would have been equitable) because the non-applicant spouse had omitted to crave such payment.

    (b)   an order for the payment of a periodical allowance to him by the other party to the marriage;

    (c)   an incidental order within the meaning of section 14(2) of this Act."

Any such order, defined in the Act as "an order for financial provision,"[24] is essentially discretionary and is thus subject to review by an appellate court only if it can be shown that the judge of first instance misdirected himself in law or failed to take into account a relevant and material factor or reached a result which is manifestly inequitable or plainly wrong.[25] The considerations applicable to the various orders for financial provision are now considered in turn.

Orders for capital payment or transfer of property

An order for payment of a capital sum or transfer of property may be made either (a) on granting decree of divorce, or (b) within such period as the court on granting decree of divorce may specify.[26] The court may stipulate that the order will come into effect at a specified future date.[27]

The court, on making an order for payment of a capital sum, may order that the capital sum will be payable by instalments.[28]

The court is bound not to make an order for transfer of property if the consent of a third party which is necessary under any obligation, enactment or rule of law has not been obtained.[29] An order for transfer of property subject to security cannot be made

---

[24] 1985 Act, s.8(3).

[25] *Little* v. *Little*, 1990 S.L.T. 785 at pp. 786 and 787 and *Peacock* v. *Peacock*, 1994 S.L.T. 40.

[26] *Ibid.*, s.12(1). The only way in which the court can give effect to s.12(1)(b) is to order a proof on a specified day; adjournment of that diet has no effect on the court's power to make the orders—*Mackin* v. *Mackin*, 1991 S.L.T. (Sh.Ct.) 22.

[27] s.12(2). See *e.g. Little, supra* (payment postponed in part until after expected date of sale of matrimonial home), *Dorrian* v. *Dorrian*, 1991 S.C.L.R. 661 and *Gulline* v. *Gulline*, 1992 S.L.T. (Sh.Ct.) 71 (payment postponed in each case until date of vesting of pension entitlement) and *Shand* v. *Shand*, 1994 S.L.T. 387 (payment postponed until likely date of conclusion of defender's sequestration).

[28] s.12(3). "Instalment payments may well be appropriate when the capital asset concerned is an income-generating asset. Where there is no such capital asset, for the court to require capital to be created by payment of instalments arising out of income would be quite wrong and contrary to the intention of the Act. To do so would merely be to establish a requirement to pay a periodical allowance for a very extended period but under another name." (*Dorrian cit. supra*, at p. 663D). A capital sum payable by instalments was awarded in *Kelly* v. *Kelly*, 1992 G.W.D. 36–2130.

[29] s.15(1).

without the consent of the creditor unless he has had an opportunity of being heard by the court.[30] Where the consent of a third party to such a transfer is necessary by virtue of an obligation, enactment or rule of law, or the property is subject to a security, intimation must be made to the third party or creditor, as the case may be.[31]

Application for an order for a capital payment or transfer of property[32] may be made by the pursuer by inserting a crave therefor in the initial writ; and by the defender by inserting a crave in the defences.[33]

Where an application for an order under section 8(1)(*a*) or (*aa*) has been made, the court must make such order, if any, as is:

> "(*a*) justified by the principles set out in section 9 of [the] Act; and
>
> (*b*) reasonable having regard to the resources of the parties."[34]

---

[30] s.15(2).

[31] See Chap. 1, text accompanying n. 19.

[32] " ... a sufficient description of the property should be included in the order which is to be made under section [12(1)(aa)] to satisfy the requirement of the common law, which is to distinguish the subjects from all other lands. In most cases a brief description will be all that is needed. In more complex cases it may be necessary for a more detailed description to be given. The court will expect to be provided with sufficient information by the party who seeks the order to enable this to be done." (*per* Lord President Hope in *Walker* v. *Walker*, 1991 S.L.T. 157 at 160B–C). It is to be noted that the issue of whether a transfer of property order (i) is an order which itself transfers the property to the other spouse, or (ii) is no more than an order that the spouse having the title to the property should transfer it to the other (see 1986 S.L.T. (News) 97 and 1990 J.L.S. 52) has been decided by *Walker* in favour of the latter proposition. A crave for a transfer of property order requires to be framed accordingly (see App. I, text accompanying n. 21).

[33] rr. 33.48(1)(*a*) and (2)(*a*) and 33.34(1)(*b*)(ii) and (2)(*b*).

[34] 1985 Act, s.8(2), subject to ss.12 to 15 of the Act, noted *infra*. These requirements are cumulative with the result that unless both are satisfied the court has no power to make an order (*Wallis, supra,* at p. 1352F). Accordingly, s.8(2)(*b*) does not entitle the court to award any greater amount by way of a capital sum beyond what is justified by the principles set forth in the Act but "can only operate to cut down any sum, otherwise justified, having regard to the current resources of the parties" (*Latter* v. *Latter*, 1990 S.L.T. 805 at p. 807). Orders for financial provision were refused because they were not reasonable having regard to the resources of the defender in *McKenna* v. *McKenna*, unreported. Regard was had to the payee's resources in *Macdonald* v. *Macdonald*, 1993 S.C.L.R. 132. The following observations as to the interaction of s.8 (2)(*b*) and s.9(1)(*a*) are to be found in the speech of Lord Keith of Kinkel in *Wallis, supra,* at p. 1351F–L:

> "There can be no doubt that for the purposes of the division contemplated by s 9 (1)(a) the matrimonial property is to be valued as at the relevant date

Section 9(1) specifies the principles which the court must apply in deciding what order for financial provision, if any, to make. These are:

> "(*a*) the net value of the matrimonial property should be shared fairly between the parties to the marriage [Principle A];
>
> (*b*) fair account should be taken of any economic advantage derived by either party from contributions by the other, and of any economic disadvantage suffered by either party in the interests of the other party or the family [Principle B];
>
> (*c*) any economic burden of caring, after divorce, for a child of

and in the absence of special circumstances the net value as at that date is to be divided equally between the parties. It is clear, moreover, that the Act does nothing to address directly the problems which may arise where some item of matrimonial property has increased or fallen in value during the period since the relevant date, though some of these problems may be capable of being solved by application of s. 8(2)(*b*). For example, if the matrimonial home, being held in the sole name of one of the parties, were to be destroyed by fire uninsured after the relevant date but before the date of the proof, the party who owned the property might be required to pay the other party half its value at the relevant date if his or her total resources at the date of the proof were sufficient to make it reasonable for such payment to be made, but not if the party in question had no significant resources. Similar considerations could apply where the property in question consisted in a block of shares which had fallen dramatically in value. Further, it would seem to make no difference in principle that the property in question was at the relevant date owned jointly by the parties or indeed by a party who, in contrast to the other, was lacking in resources at the date of the proof. It might well be not only justified by the principle in s 9 (1)(a) but also reasonable under s 8 (2)(b) that the better off party should pay to the worse off one half of the value of the property at the relevant date in exchange for the latter's devalued interest at the date of the proof.

A more intractable problem would arise in the situation where matrimonial property wholly owned by one party had depreciated substantially in value between the relevant date and the date of the proof but at the latter date the party owning it had no other resources. An equal division as at the relevant date involving payment by the party owning the property to the other party of one half of the net value at the relevant date would result in the latter party receiving very much more than the former party would be left with, which might indeed be nothing at all. It does not appear that s 8 (2)(b) could be applied in such a way as to redress the balance in a situation of that kind. The solution might be found in a finding of special circumstances under s 10 (1), though changes in the value of matrimonial property between the relevant date and the date of the proof can hardly, perhaps, be regarded as so unusual as to amount to special circumstances. It is for consideration whether amending legislation is required to enable courts to deal with the kind of problems I have indicated in such a way as to produce fair results."

the marriage under the age of 16 years should be shared
fairly between the parties [Principle C];

(d) a party who has been dependent to a substantial degree on
the financial support of the other party should be awarded
such financial provision as is reasonable to enable him to
adjust, over a period of not more than three years from the
date of the decree of divorce, to the loss of that support on
divorce [Principle D];

(e) a party who at the time of the divorce seems likely to suffer
serious financial hardship as a result of the divorce should
be awarded such financial provision as is reasonable to
relieve him of hardship over a reasonable period [Principle
E]."

The principles are at this juncture considered individually in
relation to other provisions of the Act respecting their application.

Principle A. *The net value of the matrimonial property* should be
shared fairly between the parties to the marriage.

(i) *The matrimonial property* is all the property[35] belonging to the
parties or either of them at the relevant date[36] which was acquired
by them or him (otherwise than by way of gift[37] or succession from
a third party) either (a) before the marriage for use by them as a
family home or as furniture or plenishings for such home, or (b)
during the marriage but before the relevant date.[38] Property must
fall within (a) or (b) to constitute matrimonial property.[39]

The proportion of any rights or interests of either party under a

---

[35] Such may be heritable *or* moveable property (*Petrie* v. *Petrie*, 1988 S.C.L.R. 390).
As to the former, see *Smith* v. *Smith*, 1992 G.W.D. 23–1324.

[36] The "relevant date" is whichever is the earlier of (i) the date on which the parties
ceased to cohabit; and (ii) the date of service of the summons (*sic*) in the action
for divorce—s.10(3). (The Scottish Law Commission in their *Report on Family
Law* (Scot. Law Com. No. 135, 1992) propose an amendment to s.10(3) by adding
after the word "summons" the words "or initial writ"). The parties to a
marriage are held to cohabit with one another only when they are in fact living
together as man and wife (s.27(2)), as to which see Chap. 3, n. 42 and *Buczynska*
v. *Buczynski*, 1989 S.L.T. 558. No account is to be taken of any cessation of
cohabitation where the parties thereafter resumed cohabitation (except where
the parties ceased to cohabit for a continuous period of 90 days or more before
resuming cohabitation for a period or periods of less than 90 days in all)—s.10
(7). As to s.10(7), see *Pryde* v. *Pryde*, 1991 S.L.T. (Sh.Ct.) 26.

[37] As to "gift", see *Whittome* v. *Whittome*, 1993 S.C.L.R. 137; 1994 S.L.T. 114.

[38] s.10(4).

[39] *Maclellan* v. *Maclellan*, 1988 S.C.L.R. 399 (croft tenancy acquired prior to
marriage for use other than as family home not matrimonial property (but *cf.*
obiter dicta in *Buczynska, supra*, at p. 560)).

life policy or occupational pension scheme[40] or similar arrangement referable to the period between the date of the marriage and the relevant date is taken to form part of the matrimonial property.[41] A claim for damages in respect of an accident which occurred after the date of the marriage but before the relevant date has been held to be matrimonial property.[42] Shares in a private company issued during the period between the date of the marriage and the relevant date and derived from a series of gifted shareholdings in five companies, which had become subsidiaries of the company following upon an overall reconstruction, have been held to be matrimonial property.[43] Shares in a private company allotted as a bonus issue during the period between the date of the marriage and the relevant date in respect of a gifted shareholding have been held not to be matrimonial property, as have the shares in the public company the registration and flotation of which resulted from the reorganisation of that same private company.[44] A matrimonial home bought in a party's name prior to the date of the marriage with funds given by that party's relatives to her solicitors prior to settlement has been held not to be matrimonial property.[45] A redundancy payment received after the relevant date has been held not to be matrimonial property.[46] A payment received upon leaving the army after the relevant date has been held not to be matrimonial property.[47]

(ii) *The net value* of the matrimonial property is the value[48] of the property at the relevant date after deduction of any debts,[49]

---

[40] An interest in an armed forces pension scheme is matrimonial property (*Thomson* v. *Thomson*, 1991 S.C.L.R. 655).

[41] s.10(5).

[42] *Skarpaas* v. *Skarpaas*, 1993 S.L.T. 343 (see also *Petrie, cit. supra*).

[43] *Latter* v. *Latter*, 1990 S.L.T. 805.

[44] *Whittome* v. *Whittome, cit. supra*.

[45] *Latter, cit. supra*.

[46] *Smith* v. *Smith*, 1989 S.L.T. 668 and *Tyrrell* v. *Tyrrell*, 1990 S.L.T. 406.

[47] *Gibson* v. *Gibson*, 1990 G.W.D. 4–213.

[48] Where the parties have not agreed the value of an item of matrimonial property, the court may only make a finding as to such value by reference to the evidence, which failing by selecting a figure falling within the parties' respective estimates—*Pryde* v. *Pryde*, 1991 S.L.T. (Sh.Ct.) 26 and *Fleming* v. *Fleming*, 1993 G.W.D. 9–621.

[49] The income tax due on income earned up to the relevant date is a debt which falls to be deducted irrespective of the Inland Revenue's system of recovery (*Buchan* v. *Buchan*, 1992 S.C.L.R. 766), but any contingent tax liability that might emerge in the event of accrued interest due to a party being paid at some time in the future is not such a debt (*McConnell* v. *McConnell*, 1993 G.W.D. 34–2185). It

outstanding at that date, incurred by the parties or either of
them (a) before the marriage so far as they relate to the
matrimonial property, and (b) during the marriage.[50]
Any changes in value after the relevant date must be left out
of account when calculating the value of the matrimonial
property.[51]

The rights or interests of a party under a life policy may be
valued on the basis of its surrender value or on the basis of its
replacement value.[52] The rights or interests of a party under an
occupational pension scheme may be valued on the basis of a
continuing service value rather than on the basis of a leaving
service value.[53] A claim for damages which is yet to be quantified
and admitted may be valued on the basis that it will attract less if
offered for sale in the market place than the amount awarded by

has been held that capital gains tax exigible on a notional realisation of
matrimonial property at the relevant date does not fall to be taken into account
(*former, supra* at p. 809, *McConnell, supra*).

[50] s.10(2).

[51] *Wallis* v. *Wallis*, 1992 S.L.T. 676 at p. 679F and 1994 S.L.T. 1348 at p. 1351L.

[52] "The surrender value is the amount which the insurance company is prepared
to pay to the policy holder if he wishes to cease paying premiums. The
replacement value is the amount of money which an individual would need to
invest to replace the proceeds which might reasonably have been expected to
arise from the policy." (*per* R. Watson & Sons, Consulting Actuaries, in
"Watsons Comment," April 1990). There is no reported case indicating a
judicial preference for one or other of these alternatives.

[53] "The continuing service value is based on pensionable service up to the relevant
date, but with allowance for salary increases until retirement ... [and] for the
possibility of death or leaving service before retirement. The leaving service
value also takes pensionable service up to the relevant date, but is based on
pensionable salary at that date, with allowance for subsequent increases in
deferred pensions." (*per* R. Watson & Sons, Consulting Actuaries, *loc. cit.*). The
latter was described by the Lord Ordinary in *Bannon* v. *Bannon*, 1993 S.L.T. 999
as "flawed since it assumes as the event giving rise to the final salary [the basis
upon which the defender's actual pension rights however they may emerge are
to be determined] one which is proved not to have occurred [*viz.* the defender's
leaving service]. It also fails to take into account the fact that the payments
already subscribed by the defender before the date of separation were directed
to providing cover for other and future events just as much as are payments
made by the defender after the date of separation" (at p. 1004A). The continuing
service approach was also preferred in *Muir* v. *Muir*, 1989 S.L.T. (Sh.Ct.) 20, *Little*
v. *Little*, 1989 S.C.L.R. 613 and *Gulline* v. *Gulline*, 1992 S.L.T. (Sh.Ct.) 71 (*cf. Bell* v.
Bell, 1988 S.C.L.R. 45 and *Park* v. *Park*, 1988 S.C.L.R. 885). A party's interest in a
pension scheme was valued without reference to the other spouse's interest *qua*
widow in *Brooks* v. *Brooks*, 1993 S.L.T. 184, *Bannon, supra*, and *Welsh* v. *Welsh*,
1994 G.W.D. 1–39. It has been judicially observed to be proper and useful to lead
actuarial evidence with respect to the value of pension rights—see *Brooks, supra*,

the decree which is obtained at the end of the day.[54] A business may be valued on the basis of a break-up value or a forced sale or on the basis of a value as a going concern.[55] A house may be valued with a deduction for a penalty which would have been incurred by a hypothetical early sale at the relevant date.[56] Household contents may be valued on the basis of auction room prices or on a willing buyer/willing seller basis.[57] A debt due to a party to the marriage may be valued at less than its book value.[58] The court may derive assistance from a table of matrimonial property showing values.[59]

(iii) The net value of the matrimonial property is taken to be *shared fairly* when it is shared equally or in such other proportions as are justified by special circumstances.[60]

"Special circumstances", without prejudice to the generality of the words, may include[61]:

(a) the terms of any agreement between the parties on the

---

at p. 186 C. The information required for actuarial valuations under s.10(5) is set forth in App. V. See also articles, (1991) 36 J.L.S. 45, (1991) 21 Fam. Law 258, (1993) 38 J.L.S. 348 and 1993 S.L.T. (News) 321.

[54] *Skarpaas* v. *Skarpaas*, 1993 S.L.T. 343. And see *Louden* v. *Louden*, 1994 S.L.T. 381.

[55] Businesses were valued on a going concern basis in *McKenzie* v. *McKenzie*, 1991 S.L.T. 461 and *Savage* v. *Savage*, 1993 G.W.D. 28–1779. The method of valuation of shares in private limited companies may present formidable difficulties—see *Latter* v. *Latter*, 1990 S.L.T. 805, *Crockett* v. *Crockett*, 1992 S.C.L.R. 591 and *McConnell* v. *McConnell*, 1993 G.W.D. 34–2185.

[56] *Mackin* v. *Mackin*, 1991 S.L.T. (Sh.Ct.) 22 and *Lawson* v. *Lawson*, 1993 G.W.D. 2–119.

[57] Neither method may be held strictly apposite (*Latter, cit. supra*). Note that there is a presumption of equal shares in household goods obtained in prospect of or during the marriage other than by gift or succession from a third party—1985 Act, s.25.

[58] See *Shipton* v. *Shipton*, 1992 S.C.L.R. 23.

[59] See *Crockett, supra* and App. VI.

[60] s.10(1).

[61] See *Kerrigan* v. *Kerrigan*, 1988 S.C.L.R. 603 and *White* v. *White*, 1992 S.C.L.R. 769 in each case (brevity of marriage held in each case to be a special circumstance), *Buczynska* v. *Buczynski*, 1989 S.L.T. 558 and *Wallis* v. *Wallis*, 1992 S.L.T. 676 (post-separation increase in value of matrimonial home held in each case not to be a special circumstance), *Farrell* v. *Farrell*, 1990 S.C.L.R. 717 (voluntary assumption of co-owning spouse's mortgage liability and low net value of matrimonial home held to be special circumstances), *Jesner* v. *Jesner*, 1992 S.L.T. 999 (husband's loss of household contents held to be a special circumstance), and *Wallis, cit. supra* (mere fact of transfer of property into joint names held not to be a special circumstance). See also *Clokie* v. *Clokie*, 1993 G.W.D. 16–1059 (payment of entire price of a matrimonial home 21 years prior to separation a factor of less weight than if marriage had been of relatively short duration).

ownership or division of any of the matrimonial property[62];

(b) the source of the funds or assets used to acquire any of the matrimonial property where those funds or assets were not derived from the income or efforts of the parties during the marriage[63];

(c) any destruction or dissipation[64] or alienation of property by either spouse[65];

(d) the nature of the matrimonial property, the use made of it (including use for business purposes or as a matrimonial home) and the extent to which it is reasonable to expect it to be realised or divided or used as security[66];

(e) the actual or prospective liability for any expenses of valuation or transfer of property in connection with the divorce.[67]

It is open to the court to divide a particular item of matrimonial property from the rest to meet a special circumstance which bears

---

[62] s.10(6)(*a*). See also *Anderson* v. *Anderson*, 1991 S.L.T. (Sh.Ct.) 11 and *Webster* v. *Webster*, 1992 G.W.D. 25–1432.

[63] s.10(6)(*b*); for relevant "sources" see, *e.g. Phillip* v. *Phillip*, 1988 S.C.L.R. 427 (pre-marriage house), *Kerrigan* v. *Kerrigan*, 1988 S.C.L.R. 603 (pursuer's mother), *Buczynska, cit. supra* (pursuer's mother), *Buchanan* v. *Buchanan*, 1989 G.W.D. 26–1166 (pre-marriage houses), *Budge* v. *Budge*, 1990 S.L.T. 319 (pre-marriage house), *Latter, cit. supra* (defender's family), *Jesner* v. *Jesner*, 1992 S.L.T. 999 (pre-marriage house and family trust); *Crockett* v. *Crockett*, 1992 S.C.L.R. 591 (O.H.) and unreported (I.H.) (defender's company); *Davidson* v. *Davidson*, 1993 G.W.D. 31–2000 (inheritance); *Milne* v. *Milne*, 1994 G.W.D. 11–666 (pursuer's family); and *Rae* v. *Rae*, unreported (pre-marriage house).

[64] See *Park* v. *Park*, 1988 S.C.L.R. 584 (non-payment of mortgage not dissipation).

[65] s.10(6)(*c*).

[66] s.10(6)(*d*), applied in, *e.g. Petrie* v. *Petrie*, 1988 S.C.L.R. 390 (damages award), *Muir* v. *Muir*, 1989 S.L.T. (Sh.Ct.) 20 (pension), *Cooper* v. *Cooper*, 1989 S.C.L.R. 347 (matrimonial home), *Budge* v. *Budge*, 1990 S.L.T. 319 (matrimonial home/croft), *Carpenter* v. *Carpenter*, 1990 S.L.T. (Sh.Ct.) 68 (pension), *Little* v. *Little*, 1989 S.C.L.R. 613 (O.H.) and 1990 S.L.T. 785 (I.H.) (motor cars, matrimonial home, pension), *Farrell* v. *Farrell*, 1990 S.C.L.R. 717 (matrimonial home), *Skarpaas* v. *Skarpaas*, 1991 S.L.T. (Sh.Ct.) 15 (damages claim), *Symon* v. *Symon*, 1991 S.C.L.R. 414 (pension), *McGuire* v. *McGuire's Curator Bonis*, 1991 S.L.T. (Sh.Ct.) 76 (criminal injuries compensation award), *MacQueen* v. *MacQueen*, 1992 G.W.D. 28–1653 (pension), *Crockett* v. *Crockett*, 1992 S.C.L.R. 591 (O.H.) and unreported (I.H.) (pension and shares), *Fleming* v. *Fleming*, 1993 G.W.D. 9–621 (pension), *Milne* v. *Milne*, 1994 G.W.D. 11–666 (matrimonial home), *Mainland* v. *Mainland*, unreported (pension), *Wilson* v. *Wilson*, 1993 G.W.D. 38–2521 (pension), *Peacock* v. *Peacock*, 1994 S.L.T. 40 (matrimonial home), *Bannon* v. *Bannon*, 1993 S.L.T. 999 (pension), and *Davidson* v. *Davidson*, 1993 G.W.D. 31–2000 (farm).

[67] s.10(6)(*e*).

on it primarily, there being room for the scheme of the Act to be applied in different ways in different situations as a matter of discretion.[68] Where for example special circumstances involve the nature or use of individual items of matrimonial property (see (d) *supra*), the court's discretion to take account of such nature or use extends to refraining from valuing the properties if to do so would have no practical result, or otherwise treating the items differently from others according to their nature or the use to which they are put.[69]

The question of expenses is bound up intimately with the division of the matrimonial property and the effects of that division on the parties' resources.[70]

In applying Principle A, the court must not take account of the conduct of either party unless the conduct has adversely affected the financial resources which are relevant to the decision of the court on a claim for financial provision.[71]

---

[68] *Crockett* v. *Crockett*, unreported (unequal division of value of pension interests and company shares).

[69] *Little* v. *Little*, 1990 S.L.T. 785 wherein, under reference to the interest of each party in a superannuation scheme, Lord President Hope stated (at p. 788 K): "The ... scheme provides that the member will be paid an inflation linked pension on his retirement and also a lump sum of three times the first year's pension. The values attached to each party's interest represented the actuarial value of their prospective entitlement under the scheme at the relevant date, not cash in hand. The nature of the scheme is such that neither interest will be capable of being realised for cash of equivalent value at any stage, since a substantial part of the benefit is represented by the pension. Clearly, matrimonial property of this character requires careful attention if it is to be shared fairly between the parties in a settlement on divorce, and it would be a serious error if the court were to assume that an equal and instant division of the actuarial value was capable of being made as if it were cash in hand. On the other hand there may be cases where there are other realisable assets of sufficient value which can be drawn upon to achieve that result, and if so it may well be appropriate to take the full actuarial value into account in achieving the division in the knowledge that the party who makes the payment has other resources on which he or she can draw." (Such cases include *Latter* v. *Latter*, 1990 S.L.T. 805 and *Brooks* v. *Brooks*, 1993 S.L.T. 184).

[70] *Ibid.*, at p. 790. Note the observation there made by Lord President Hope that there is much to be said for the view that on the question of expenses the parties' conduct of the litigation rather than the result itself should be the principal criterion upon which to proceed. See also *Macdonald* v. *Macdonald* (*No.2*), 1993 G.W.D. 16-1057 (approved by Extra Division, 1994 G.W.D. 7-404) and *Whittome* v. *Whittome* (*No.2*), 1994 S.L.T. 130. (*Cf. Ferguson* v. *Maclennan Salmon Co. Ltd.*, 1990 S.L.T. 428, at p. 431, with regard to minutes of tender in divorce actions.)

[71] s.11(7)(*a*).

Principle B. Fair account should be taken of any *economic advantage* derived by either party from *contributions* by the other, and of any *economic disadvantage* suffered by either party in the interests of the other party or of the family.[72]

Economic advantage means advantage gained whether before or during the marriage and includes gains in capital, in income and

---

[72] Cases in which Principle B was explicitly considered include *Petrie* v. *Petrie*, 1988 S.C.L.R. 390 (husband held not to have derived economic advantage from presence of wife in the home), *Kerrigan* v. *Kerrigan*, 1988 S.C.L.R. 603 (wife held to have derived economic advantage from husband's mortgage payments by increase in value of jointly owned matrimonial home), *Muir* v. *Muir*, 1989 S.L.T. (Sh.Ct.) 20 (husband held not to have derived economic advantage from wife's occupation of his house since separation), *Little* v. *Little*, 1989 S.C.L.R. 613 (wife held to have suffered economic disadvantage in the family interest by the interruption of her professional career in order to look after house and family for a period), *Tyrrell* v. *Tyrrell*, 1990 S.L.T. 406 (husband held not to have derived any economic advantage from any contribution by wife by increase in value of his pension since separation), *Skarpaas* v. *Skarpaas*, 1991 S.L.T. (Sh.Ct.) 15 (wife held to have suffered economic disadvantage in relation to her business because of need to look after injured husband), *Jesner* v. *Jesner*, 1992 S.L.T. 999 (husband held to have derived economic advantage from wife's contribution in looking after family home and caring for family), *Shipton* v. *Shipton*, 1992 S.C.L.R. 23 (wife held to have suffered economic disadvantage through her inability to work during the marriage), *Toye* v. *Toye*, 1992 S.C.L.R. 95 (wife held to have suffered economic disadvantage by giving up work which she could not readily resume), *Luckwell* v. *Luckwell*, 1992 G.W.D. 34–2005 (wife held to have suffered economic disadvantage where parties living in relatively remote area and wife not resuming work after children had left home), *Kelly* v. *Kelly*, 1992 G.W.D. 36–2130 (wife held to have suffered economic disadvantage: (i) as a result of giving up work to carry out home duties; and (ii) as a result of not exercising, at husband's urging, her entitlement to buy back pension rights foregone by her upon marriage), *Macdonald* v. *Macdonald*, 1992 S.C.L.R. 132 and 1994 G.W.D. 7–404 (wife held to have suffered economic disadvantage through having assumed rather greater economic burden of caring for children than husband hitherto), *Davidson* v. *Davidson*, 1993 G.W.D. 31–2000 (husband held to have derived economic advantage from gifts of money from wife), *Ranaldi* v. *Ranaldi*, unreported (husband held to have derived economic advantage through wife's having taken lodgers throughout marriage), *Louden* v. *Louden*, 1994 S.L.T. 381 (wife held to have suffered economic disadvantage by giving up work and losing earning potential) and *Welsh* v. *Welsh*, 1994 G.W.D. 1–39 (wife's economic disadvantage in giving up well paid employment to look after husband and children held to have been balanced by economic advantage from being maintained by husband and from enjoying the results of mortgage payments made exclusively by him in respect of jointly owned matrimonial home and by economic disadvantage suffered by him accordingly; but economic advantage held to have been enjoyed by husband in having exclusive use of house after separation with corresponding economic disadvantage to wife).

in earning capacity; and *economic disadvantage* is construed accordingly.[73]

Contributions are contributions made whether before or during the marriage, including indirect and non-financial contributions and, in particular, any such contribution made by looking after the family home or caring for the family.[73]

In applying this principle, the court must have regard to the extent to which:

(a) the economic advantages or disadvantages sustained by either party have been balanced by the economic advantages or disadvantages sustained by the other party; and

(b) a resulting imbalance has been or will be corrected by a sharing of the value of the matrimonial property or otherwise.[74]

The court must not, on the other hand, take account of the conduct of either party unless the conduct has adversely affected the financial resources which are relevant to the decision of the court on a claim for financial provision.[75]

Principle C. Any economic burden of caring, after divorce, for a child of the marriage under the age of 16 years should be shared fairly between the parties.[76]

---

[73] s.9(2). The Scottish Law Commission in their *Report on Family Law* (Scot. Law Com. No. 135, 1992) propose the amendment of s.9(2) by substituting reference to the parties' children for "family" and defining the parties' children as including "children treated by both of the parties as children of their family."

[74] s.11(2).

[75] s.11(7)(*a*).

[76] Cases in which Principle C was explicitly considered include *Monkman* v. *Monkman*, 1988 S.L.T. (Sh.Ct.) 37 (expenditure on child after sixteenth birthday not to be taken into account but economic burden held to be shared fairly by periodical allowance under s.9(1)(*c*) for wife until child about 20 years old), *Morrison* v. *Morrison*, 1989 S.C.L.R. 574 (economic burden held to be shared fairly by award to wife under s.9(1)(*c*) of two-thirds of value of matrimonial home and contents), *White* v. *White*, 1990 G.W.D. 12–616 (economic burden held to be shared fairly by relatively token compensation under s.9(1)(*c*) in the form of capital), *Millar* v. *Millar*, 1990 S.C.L.R. 666 (economic burden held to be shared fairly under reference to alimentary award in child's favour), *Shipton* v. *Shipton*, 1992 S.C.L.R. 23 (economic burden held to be shared fairly by award of greater share of matrimonial property), *Toye* v. *Toye*, 1992 S.C.L.R. 95 (economic burden held to be shared fairly by award of periodical allowance for three years), *Macdonald* v. *Macdonald*, 1993 S.C.L.R. 132 (economic burden held to be shared fairly by award of capital sum to enable need to provide accommodation for children to be met), *Shepherd* v. *Shepherd*, unreported (economic burden held to be shared fairly by award of periodical allowance for three years) and

In applying this principle, the court must have regard to:

(a) any decree or arrangement for aliment for the child;
(b) any expenditure or loss of earning capacity caused by the need to care for the child;
(c) the need to provide suitable accommodation for the child;
(d) the age and health of the child;
(e) the educational, financial and other circumstances of the child;
(f) the availability and cost of suitable child-care facilities or services;
(g) the needs and resources of the parties; and
(h) all the other circumstances of the case (which *may* include, if the court thinks fit, taking account of any support, financial or otherwise, given by the party who is to make the financial provision to any person whom he maintains as a dependant in his household whether or not he owes an obligation of aliment to that person).[77]

The court must not however take account of the conduct of either party unless the conduct has adversely affected the financial resources which are relevant to the decision of the court on a claim for financial provision.[78]

Principle D.   A party who has been dependent to a substantial degree on the financial support of the other party should be awarded such financial provision as is reasonable to enable him to adjust, over a period of not more than three years from the date of the decree of divorce, to the loss of that support on divorce.[79]

Mainland v. *Mainland,* unreported (economic burden held to be shared fairly by transfer of interest in matrimonial home at less than value of interest).

[77] s.11(3) and (6).

[78] s.11(7)(*a*).

[79] Cases in which Principle D was explicitly considered include *Stott* v. *Stott,* 1987 G.W.D. 17–645 (wife aged 42 years and married for 24 years, no dependent children, in low paid part-time employment and not well educated, awarded periodical allowance under s.9(1)(*d*) for maximum period of three years from date of decree and at reduced rate for a further four years under s.9(1)(*e*)), *Dever* v. *Dever,* 1988 S.C.L.R. 352 (wife aged 27 years and married and living with husband for six years, no children, in receipt of state benefits, claimed no maintenance since separation 18 months prior to diet of proof, awarded periodical allowance under s.9(1)(*d*) for six months from date of decree), *Petrie* v. *Petrie,* 1988 S.C.L.R. 390 (wife aged 42 years and married and living with husband for two years, one child, cohabited with husband for several years before marriage, in receipt of state benefits, no skills or qualifications but fit for

work, claimed no maintenance since separation in belief her adultery disentitled her, awarded periodical allowance under s.9(1)(*d*) for one year from date of decree), *Atkinson* v. *Atkinson*, 1988 S.C.L.R. 396 (wife earning salary insufficient for her upkeep in the standard of life she enjoyed during marriage awarded a periodical allowance under s.9(1)(*d*) for three years from date of decree), *Park* v. *Park*, 1988 S.C.L.R. 584 (wife married and living with husband for five years, no children, earning one-fifth of the total amount earned by the parties, awarded a periodical allowance under s.9(1)(*d*) to increase her "share" to one-third and allow her to adjust back to one-fifth, award being made for one year and at reduced rate for further year), *Muir* v. *Muir*, 1989 S.L.T. (Sh.Ct.) 20 (wife aged 47 years, no dependent children, in receipt of invalidity benefit, hoping to resume work as shop assistant, separated for four years and in receipt of maintenance during last of those years, awarded a periodical allowance under s.9(1)(*d*) for one year from date of decree), *Tyrrell* v. *Tyrrell*, 1990 S.L.T. 406 (wife married and living with husband for 18 years, in part-time employment and in receipt of maintenance for seven years after separation until date of proof, awarded a periodical allowance under s.9(1)(*d*) for one year from date of decree), *Sheret* v. *Sheret*, 1990 S.C.L.R. 799 (wife married and living with husband for two years, aged 42 years, with no immediate prospects of employment, supported only periodically by husband, awarded a periodical allowance under s.9(1)(*d*) for 13 weeks from date of decree), *Millar* v. *Millar*, 1990 S.C.L.R. 666 (wife married and living with husband for ten years, one child in joint custody, wife in part-time employment and in receipt of interim aliment for herself and child, awarded aliment in larger amount for child leaving small shortfall, held not entitled to a periodical allowance under s.9(1)(*d*)), *Thomson* v. *Thomson*, 1991 S.L.T. 126 (wife dependent wholly for her financial support on husband for five years before separation, awarded interim aliment three years later, husband held to have taken every opportunity to avoid his financial responsibilities since separation, wife awarded a periodical allowance under s.9(1)(*d*) for three years), *Barclay* v. *Barclay*, 1991 S.C.L.R. 205 (wife aged 29 years, married and living with husband for some three years, no children, permanently disabled by multiple sclerosis and resident in a nursing home, not envisaged that she would ever be able to resume life in the community, awarded a periodical allowance under s.9(1)(*d*) for three years), *Gray* v. *Gray*, 1991 S.C.L.R. 422 (wife dependent to substantial degree on husband's financial support prior to separation, since then not provided with nor had she sought financial support from husband, held to have adjusted to withdrawal of support and no award made), *Kelly* v. *Kelly*, 1992 G.W.D. 36–2130 (wife with secure job and reasonable salary held to have suffered loss of support, account taken of fact equal sharing of matrimonial property not possible and of wife's need to build up pension fund, wife awarded a periodical allowance under s.9(1)(*d*) for three years), *Murray* v. *Murray*, 1993 G.W.D. 16–1058 (wife aged 56 years, married and living with husband for 26 years, in part-time employment but held not to have sought to decrease her dependence on husband through choice, due to retire at the age of 60, held entitled to a further short period to adjust to loss of husband's support, awarded a periodical allowance under s.9(1)(*d*) for two years), *Louden* v. *Louden*, 1994 S.L.T. 381 (wife aged 45 years, married and living with husband for 17 years, one child (aged 17), wife unemployed and requiring to retrain to "get back on employment ladder" awarded a periodical allowance under s.9(1)(*d*) for one year), *McConnell* v. *McConnell*, 1993 G.W.D. 34–2185 (wife married and living with husband for 16 years, three children, wife almost exclusively dependent

In applying this principle, the court must have regard to:

(a) the age, health and earning capacity of the party who is claiming the financial provision;

(b) the duration and extent of the dependence of that party prior to divorce[80];

(c) any intention of that party to undertake a course of education or training;[81]

(d) the needs and resources of the parties; and

(e) all the other circumstances of the case (which *may* include, if the court thinks fit, taking account of any support, financial or otherwise, given by the party who is to make the financial provision to any person whom he maintains as a dependant in his household whether or not he owes an obligation of aliment to that person).[82]

The court must not, however, take account of the conduct of either party unless either (a) the conduct has adversely affected the financial resources which are relevant to the decision of the court on a claim for financial provision, or (b) it would be manifestly inequitable to leave the conduct out of account.[83]

Principle E. A party who at the time of the divorce seems likely to suffer serious financial hardship as a result of the divorce should be awarded such financial provision as is reasonable to relieve him of hardship over a reasonable period.[84]

---

upon income from husband, held reasonable for her to have period of time to adjust to new circumstances created by determination of the litigation, awarded a periodical allowance under s.9(1)(*d*) for three years), *Shepherd* v. *Shepherd*, unreported (wife aged about 40 years, married and living with husband for less than two years, with two children of her own, had given up satisfactory job abroad to join husband, awarded a periodical allowance under s.9(1)(*d*) for three years) and *Wilson* v. *Wilson*, 1993 G.W.D. 38–2521 (wife a qualified vet but unable so to work by reason of commitments to parties' children, had applied for teacher training course, awarded a periodical allowance under s.9(1)(*d*) for one year).

[80] Dependence prior to the marriage may be taken into account *Petrie* v. *Petrie*, 1988 S.C.L.R. 390. Failure to seek financial support after separation may disentitle the claimant to an award under s.9(1)(*d*)—*Gray* v. *Gray*, 1991 S.C.L.R. 422.

[81] The absence of any such intention has been held not to be relevant (*Stott* v. *Stott*, G.W.D. 17–647).

[82] s.11(4) and (6).

[83] s.11(7)(*a*) and (*b*).

[84] Cases in which the application of Principle E was explicitly considered include *Stott* v. *Stott*, 1987 G.W.D. 17–645 (wife aged 42 years and married for 24 years, no dependent children, in low paid part-time employment and not well

educated, awarded periodical allowance under s.9(1)(*d*) for maximum period of three years from date of decree and at reduced rate for a further four years under s.9(1)(*e*)), *Atkinson* v. *Atkinson*, 1988 S.C.L.R. 396 (wife earning salary insufficient for her upkeep in the standard of life she enjoyed during marriage but her income, and substantial capital, made it "quite out of the question" to make award under s.9(1)(*e*)), *Bell* v. *Bell*, 1988 S.C.L.R. 457 (wife aged 51 years, married and living with husband for 26 years, no dependent children, a qualified teacher but a full-time housewife and mother dependent on husband's support throughout the marriage, unlikely to find work affording reasonable remuneration, with sufficient capital to retain a nice house but with no income after divorce, awarded a periodical allowance under s.9(1)(*e*) until husband's sixtieth birthday or her own death or remarriage), *Muir* v. *Muir*, 1989 S.L.T. (Sh.Ct.) 20 (wife aged 47 years, no dependent children, in receipt of invalidity benefit, hoping to resume work as shop assistant, separated for four years and in receipt of maintenance during last of those years, awarded a periodical allowance under s.9(1)(*d*) for one year from date of decree but s.9(1)(*e*) held inapplicable), *Tyrrell* v. *Tyrrell*, 1990 S.L.T. 406 (wife married and living with husband for 18 years, in part-time employment and in receipt of maintenance for seven years after separation until date of proof, had received substantial capital at time of separation with further capital sum upon decree, held entitled to award of periodical allowance under s.9(1)(*d*) but to no award under s.9(1) (*e*)), *Johnstone* v. *Johnstone*, 1990 S.L.T. (Sh.Ct.) 79 (wife aged 35 years, married and living with husband for 13 years, 1 child, unfit for work because of epilepsy, awarded a periodical allowance until her death or remarriage under s.9(1)(*e*)), *McKenzie* v. *McKenzie*, 1991 S.L.T. 461 (wife aged nearly 60 years, married and living with husband for 16 years, no dependent children, ran small business with low income with possibility of income from lodger, entitled to small pension at 60, held liable to be "seriously short of money" notwithstanding award of capital sum if no maintenance awarded, awarded a periodical allowance until death or remarriage), *Barclay* v. *Barclay*, 1991 S.C.L.R. 205 (wife aged 29 years, married and living with husband for some three years, no children, permanently disabled by multiple sclerosis and resident in a nursing home, not envisaged that she would ever be able to resume life in the community, awarded a periodical allowance under s.9(1)(*d*) for three years from date of decree but, requiring substantial support anyway from public funds, given no award under s.9(1)(*e*)), *Kelly* v. *Kelly*, 1992 G.W.D. 36–2130 (wife with secure job and reasonable salary held entitled to award of a periodical allowance under s.9(1)(*d*) but could not be said to be likely to suffer serious financial hardship within s.9(1)(*e*)), *Murray* v. *Murray*, 1993 G.W.D. 16-1058 (wife aged 56 years, married and living with husband for 26 years, in part-time employment with the prospect of retirement on very small income at the age of 60, held entitled to award of a periodical allowance under s.9(1)(*d*), accepted as being liable to suffer financial hardship thereafter but such held not likely to be "serious" and award under s.9(1)(*e*) refused), *Savage* v. *Savage*, 1993 G.W.D. 28–1779 (wife unfit for work and unlikely to find employment but awarded a "not insubstantial" capital sum, husband's business drawings at very modest level, no award under s.9(1)(*e*)) and *Davidson* v. *Davidson*, 1993 G.W.D. 31–2000 (husband aged 46 years with very restricted earning capacity and without sound mental health, wife a very wealthy woman, marriage of five years' duration, husband awarded capital under s.9(1)(*e*) in respect of loss of home and "considerable financial comfort" of wife's money).

In applying this principle, the court must have regard to:

(a)   the age, health and earning capacity of the party who is claiming the financial provision;

(b)   the duration of the marriage;

(c)   the standard of living of the parties during the marriage;

(d)   the needs and resources of the parties; and

(e)   all the other circumstances of the case (which *may* include, if the court thinks fit, taking account of any support, financial or otherwise, given by the party who is to make the financial provision to any person whom he maintains as a dependant in his household whether or not he owes an obligation of aliment to that person).[85]

The court must not, though, take account of the conduct of either party unless either (a) the conduct has adversely affected the financial resources which are relevant to the decision of the court on a claim for financial provision, or (b) it would be manifestly inequitable to leave the conduct out of account.[86]

Where any parties have reached agreement in relation to an order for financial provision, a joint minute may be entered into expressing that agreement; and the sheriff may grant decree in respect of those parts of the joint minute in relation to which he could otherwise make an order, whether or not such a decree would include a matter for which there was no crave.[87] A joint minute is binding on the parties and cannot be set aside by the court unless: (1) the interests of third parties, such as the child of the marriage, are affected; (2) it is void or voidable on some ground applicable to the general law of contract; or (3) there is specific statutory provision to that effect.[88]

In relation to (3), section 16(1)(*b*) and (2)(*b*) of the Family Law (Scotland) Act 1985 provides that where the parties to a marriage have entered into an agreement[89] as to the financial provision to be made on divorce, the court may on granting decree of divorce[90]

---

[85] s.11(5) and (6).

[86] s.11(7)(*a*) and (*b*).

[87] r. 33.26(*c*).

[88] *Anderson* v. *Anderson*, 1989 S.C.L.R. 475. See also cases cited therein, *Sochart* v. *Sochart*, 1988 S.L.T. 799, *Horton* v. *Horton*, 1992 S.L.T. (Sh.Ct.) 37 and *Jongejan* v. *Jongejan*, 1993 S.L.T. 595 (*cf. Davidson* v. *Davidson*, 1989 S.L.T. 466 and *Stewart* v. *Stewart*, 1990 S.C.L.R. 360).

[89] "Agreement" means an agreement entered into before or after the commencement of the 1985 Act—s.16(5). An agreement recorded in a joint minute falls within s.16(1)(*b*)—*Jongejan* v. *Jongejan*, 1993 S.L.T. 595.

[90] While the court cannot make the order prior to granting decree of divorce, a preliminary proof on a crave for such an order is competent—*Gillon* v. *Gillon*,

(or within such time thereafter as the court may specify on granting decree of divorce) make an order setting aside or varying the agreement or any term of it where the agreement was not fair and reasonable at the time it was entered into.[91] Any term of an agreement purporting to exclude the right to apply for an order under section 16(1)(*b*) is void.[92] Application for the order must be made by a crave in the initial writ or defences, as the case may be.[93]

Orders for periodical allowance

An order for payment of a periodical allowance may be made on granting decree of divorce or within such period as the court on granting decree of divorce may specify.[94]

The order may be for a definite or indefinite period or until the happening of a specified event.[95] The order in any event ceases to have effect on the remarriage or death of the party receiving payment, except in relation to arrears due under it.[96] If the order is

---

1994 G.W.D. 1–42.

[91] In considering whether or not the agreement was fair and reasonable at the time it was entered into "... the court has to look at all the circumstances prior to and at the time that the agreement was entered into and relevant to its negotiation and signing, to see whether there was some unfair or unconscionable advantage taken of some factor or of some relationship between the parties which enables the court to say that an agreement was not truly entered into by one party or the other as a free agent and that the agreement or any term of it was not in the circumstances fair and reasonable at the time it was entered into. In this determination, the extent of a party's professional qualifications and experience and the nature of any advice received from a professional source may well be important factors to bear in mind in the judgment of what is fair and reasonable. Nevertheless, they cannot in themselves be determinative of the issue where other circumstances suggesting unfair advantage or unreasonable conduct by one party to influence the other in the signing of an agreement which in its terms expressly surrenders rights which that other party would have on divorce are averred ..." (*McAfee* v. *McAfee*, 1990 S.C.L.R. 805 at p. 808; the order was refused after proof—Lord Cameron of Lochbroom, June 3, 1993, unreported.) See also *Anderson* v. *Anderson*, 1991 S.L.T. (Sh.Ct.) 11, *Young* v. *Young (No. 2)*, 1991 S.L.T. 869, *Gillon, supra*, and *Worth* v. *Worth*, 1993 G.W.D. 40-2666.

[92] s.16(4).

[93] rr. 33.48(1)(*a*) and (2)(*b*).

[94] s.13(1)(*a*) and (*b*). As to s.13(1)(*b*), see *Mackin* v. *Mackin*, 1991 S.L.T. (Sh.Ct.) 22 (n. 26 *supra*). The order may also be made after the granting of decree of divorce (as to which, see n. 20 *infra* and accompanying text).

[95] s.13(3). A party is entitled to argue for a restriction in the duration of an order without having given advance notice of the intention so to contend (*Robertson* v. *Robertson*, 1989 S.C.L.R. 71).

[96] s.13(7)(*b*).

subsisting at the death of the party making the payment, it continues to operate against that party's estate.[97]

Application for an order for periodical allowance may be made in similar fashion to an application for a capital payment or transfer of property, except that the applicant's pleadings must contain an averment stating whether and, if so, when and by whom, a maintenance order has been granted in favour of or against that party or of any other person in respect of whom the order is sought.[98] The court cannot make such an order *unless* (i) the order is justified by Principle C, D or E (detailed *supra*) and (ii) it is satisfied that an order for payment of a capital sum or for transfer of property would be inappropriate or insufficient to satisfy the requirements of section 8(2) of the Act (namely that the order be justified by the principles in section 9 and be reasonable having regard to the resources of the parties).[99] The claimant must aver and prove that these conditions are satisfied,[1] even in an undefended action.[2] The rules of law and procedure concerning agreements anent capital payment or transfer of property[3] apply also to agreements anent periodical allowance, with the addition that the court has extra powers to vary the terms of an agreement relating to periodical

---

[97] s.13(7)(*a*), subject to the court's powers under s.13(4) (n. 21, *infra*).

[98] Text accompanying n. 33 *supra* and r. 33.5.

[99] s.13(2). Cases in which a periodical allowance has been awarded include *Stott* v. *Stott*, 1987 G.W.D. 17–645 (for three years with an award at a reduced rate for a further four years), *Monkman* v. *Monkman*, 1988 S.L.T. (Sh.Ct.) 37 (for 10 years), *Dever* v. *Dever*, 1988 S.C.L.R. 352 (for six months), *Petrie* v. *Petrie*, 1988 S.C.L.R. 390 (for one year), *Atkinson* v. *Atkinson*, 1988 S.C.L.R. 396 (for three years), *Bell* v. *Bell*, 1988 S.C.L.R. 457 (until death or remarriage of pursuer or sixtieth birthday of defender), *Park* v. *Park*, 1988 S.C.L.R. 584 (for one year with an award at a reduced rate for a further year), *Daley* v. *Daley*, 1988 G.W.D. 3–118 (for two years), *McDevitt* v. *McDevitt*, 1988 S.C.L.R. 206 (for three years), *Muir* v. *Muir*, 1989 S.L.T. (Sh.Ct.) 20 (for one year), *Tyrrell* v. *Tyrrell*, 1990 S.L.T. 406 (for one year), *Johnstone* v. *Johnstone*, 1990 S.L.T. (Sh.Ct.) 79 (until death or remarriage), *Sheret* v. *Sheret*, 1990 S.C.L.R. 799 (for 13 weeks), *Thomson* v. *Thomson*, 1991 S.L.T. 126 (for three years), *McKenzie* v. *McKenzie*, 1991 S.L.T. 461 (until death or remarriage), *Barclay* v. *Barclay*, 1991 S.C.L.R. 205 (for three years), *Toye* v. *Toye*, 1992 S.C.L.R. 95 (for three years), *Kelly* v. *Kelly*, 1992 G.W.D. 36–2130 (for three years), *Shepherd* v. *Shepherd*, unreported (for three years), *Louden* v. *Louden*, 1994 S.L.T. 381 (for one year) and *McConnell* v. *McConnell*, 1993 G.W.D. 34–2185 (for three years).

[1] *Mackin* v. *Mackin*, 1991 S.L.T. (Sh.Ct.) 22. See also *Savage* v. *Savage*, 1993 G.W.D. 28–1779.

[2] *Thirde* v. *Thirde*, 1987 S.C.L.R. 335 (*cf. Main* v. *Main*, 1988 G.W.D. 24–1036).

[3] See nn. 87 to 93 and accompanying text, *supra*.

allowance in certain specified circumstances.[4]

Incidental orders

"An incidental order" is defined by section 14(2) as one or more of the following orders:
- (a) an order for the sale[5] of property[6];
- (b) an order for the valuation[7] of property;
- (c) an order determining any dispute between the parties to the marriage as to their respective property rights by means of a declarator thereof or otherwise;
- (d) an order regulating the occupation of the matrimonial home or the use of furniture and plenishings therein or excluding either party to the marriage from such occupation[8];
- (e) an order regulating liability, as between the parties, for outgoings in respect of the matrimonial home or furniture or plenishings therein[9];
- (f) an order that security shall be given for any financial provision[10];
- (g) an order that payments shall be made or property transferred to any curator bonis or trustee or other person for the benefit of the party to the marriage by whom or on whose behalf application has been made under section

---

[4] See 1985 Act, s.16(1)(*a*) and (2)(*a*) and (3). See also *Mills* v. *Mills*, 1990 S.C.L.R. 213 and *Ellerby* v. *Ellerby*, 1991 S.C.L.R. 608 and r. 33.52.

[5] The order requires to be, at least principally, aimed at financial provision on divorce, so that it cannot be granted just to save the pursuer the trouble of raising a separate action for division and sale (*Reynolds* v. *Reynolds*, 1991 S.C.L.R. 175).

[6] "Property" in s.14 can only refer to such property as is properly encompassed within the ambit of the Act, *i.e.* the property of one or other or both of the parties to the marriage—*Demarco* v. *Demarco*, 1990 S.C.L.R. 635 (order for valuation of property owned by company of which defender was a shareholder refused).

[7] *cf. McKeown* v. *McKeown*, 1988 S.C.L.R. and *Demarco, supra.*

[8] So long as such an incidental order remains in force, the former spouse is deemed to be, except to the extent that the order otherwise provides, a non-entitled spouse with occupancy rights in the property as regards (i) certain general powers of management in relation thereto and (ii) protection against certain arrangements intended to defeat those rights (see s.14(5)). An order under s.14(2)(*d*) was granted in *Little* v. *Little*, Lord Cameron of Lochbroom, May 24, 1990, unreported (on this point), whereby a period of "protected occupation" for one year from the date of decree of divorce was allowed; and in *Symon* v. *Symon*, 1991 S.C.L.R. 414.

[9] See *Little, cit. supra* (order refused in *hoc statu*) and *Macdonald* v. *Macdonald (No.2)*, 1993 G.W.D. 16-1057.

[10] See *Macdonald, supra.*

8(1) of the Act;

(h) an order setting aside or varying any term in an antenuptial or postnuptial marriage settlement[11];

(j) an order as to the date from which any interest on any amount awarded shall run[12];

(k) any ancillary order which is expedient to give effect to the principles set out in section 9 of the Act or to any order made under section 8(2) of the Act.[13]

Orders (d) and (e) may only be made on or after the granting of decree of divorce; other incidental orders may be made before, on

---

[11] "Settlement" includes a settlement by way of a policy of assurance to which s.2 of the Married Women's Policies of Assurance (Scotland) Act 1880 relates.

[12] "[T]he purpose of s.14(2)(j) is to enable the court to award interest on the whole, or any part, of any amount awarded as a financial provision as from such date as it thinks appropriate, even although this may be a date earlier than the date of payment in terms of the decree.... [If] an order for interest is to be made as an incidental order under s.14(2)(j) it must, as s.8(2) provides, be justified by the principles set out in s.9 of the Act and be reasonable having regard to the resources of the parties. It should therefore be seen as an integral part of the order for financial provision, and not as something which is to be added on afterwards once all the exercises to arrive at this provision are complete. The order must also be made having regard to the purpose for which interest is awarded by the court. ... What [the court] is required to do, when the capital sum is awarded with reference to the net value of the matrimonial property, is to share fairly the net value of all the matrimonial property as at the relevant date. In most cases this will be the date of the final separation: see s.10(3)(a). There may be circumstances where a party who has had the sole use or possession of an asset since the relevant date, the whole or part of the value of which is to be shared with the other party on divorce, should be required to pay interest as consideration for the use or possession which he has had between the relevant date and the date of decree. An order for interest may, for example, be appropriate where the use or possession has resulted in a benefit which has not been taken into account in some other way in making the order for financial provision. It may also be appropriate where ... the amount of the principal sum is fixed by the decree but payment of it, in whole or in part, is postponed to a later date. Whether interest should be awarded on this basis, and if so on what part of the award, from what date and what the rate of interest should be is in the discretion of the court, bearing in mind that an incidental order for interest under s.14(2)(j) is an integral part of the order for financial provision under s.8(2) of the Act." (per Lord President Hope in *Geddes* v. *Geddes*, 1993 S.L.T. 494 at pp. 499 I–J and 500 L – 501 B). In *Savage* v. *Savage*, 1993 G.W.D. 28–1779 the Lord Ordinary awarded a lump sum under the head of interest to date of decree. In *Welsh* v. *Welsh*, 1994 G.W.D. 1–39 the Lord Ordinary awarded interest from the relevant date upon the applicant's share of the equity in the matrimonial home as valued at that date, the non-applicant spouse having had exclusive occupation thereof since the relevant date.

[13] See *Little*, *cit. supra* (order made regarding conveyancing expenses) and *McConnell* v. *McConnell*, 1993 G.W.D. 34–2185 (order made requiring defender to arrange for discharge of debt secured over matrimonial home).

or after the granting or refusal of decree of divorce.[14]

Neither an incidental order, nor any rights conferred by such an order, prejudices any rights of any third party in so far as those rights existed immediately before the making of the order.[15]

Section 14 of the 1985 Act gives the court a discretionary power, to be exercised in the circumstances of a particular case.[16] The phrase "an incidental order" means what it says, namely something done by way of order incidental or ancillary to the making of an order under section 8(2) in relation to an order under section 8(1)(*a*), (*aa*) or (*b*).[17]

ORDERS MADE AFTER THE GRANTING OF DECREE

Ordinary cause rule 33.51 provides that certain applications after decree relative to orders for financial provision require to be made by minute lodged in the process of the action to which the application relates. The applications thus provided for include[18] applications:

(a) after final decree for—

   (i) variation of the date or method of payment of a capital sum or the date of transfer of property[19];

   (ii) payment by one party to the marriage to the other of a periodical allowance[20];

   (iii) variation or recall of an order for a periodical

---

[14] s.14(1) and (3). As to the mode of application for an incidental order in a depending action, see n. 12 *supra*.

[15] s.15(3).

[16] *McKeown, cit. supra, Little, cit. supra.*

[17] *Demarco, cit. supra.*

[18] r. 33.51 (1)(*a*)(ii) bears to provide for applications for a capital sum or transfer of property order under s.12 (1)(*b*) of the 1985 Act (which enables such orders to be made within such period as the court on granting decree of divorce may specify). It is submitted that s.12 (1)(*b*) presupposes application prior to decree for any such order; and that therefore the rule is erroneous (see also n. 26 *supra*; *cf.* s.13 (1)(*b*) and (*c*)).

[19] s.12 (4), requiring that there has since the date of decree been a material change of circumstances.

[20] s.13(1)(*c*), requiring that there has, since the date of decree, been a change of circumstances. In their *Report on Family Law* (Scot. Law Com. No. 135, 1992) the Scottish Law Commission propose an amendment to the provision so as to require a *material* change of circumstances. As to an order setting aside or varying any term of an agreement relating to a periodical allowance in terms of s.16 (1)(*a*) of the 1985 Act, see (second) n. 5 *supra*.

    allowance[21];
 (iv) conversion of such an order into an order for
   payment of a capital sum or for a transfer of
   property[22]; or
 (b) after the grant or refusal of an application for—
  (i) an incidental order[23];
  (ii) variation or recall of an incidental order.[24]

Where a minute is lodged, any party may apply by motion for any interim order which may be made pending the determination of the application.[25]

---

[21] s.13(4)(*a*) requiring that since the date of the order there has been a material change of circumstances. Such change is not constituted merely by showing that the court at the time of the earlier award proceeded upon a particular hypothesis which has turned out to be incorrect—*Walker* v. *Walker*, Second Division, March 25, 1994, unreported. The application may be made by the executor of a party to the former marriage—*ibid.* (see e.g. *Sandison's Extrx.* v. *Sandison*, 1984 S.L.T. 111 and *Finlayson* v. *Finlayson's Extrx.*, 1986 S.L.T. 19). The court has power to backdate such variation or recall (s.13 (4)(*b*)) and in that event to order repayment—s.13 (6). A request for backdating was refused in *Marshall* v. *Marshall*, unreported.

[22] s.13 (4)(*c*).

[23] s.14 (1).

[24] s.14 (4), requiring that cause be shown for the variation or recall.

[25] r. 33.51 (2).

SPECIMEN CRAVES AND ASSOCIATED PLEAS-IN-LAW

1. MERITS

C— (i) To divorce the defender from the pursuer on the ground that the marriage has broken down irretrievably as established by the defender's adultery.[1]

  (ii) To divorce the defender from the pursuer on the ground that the marriage has broken down irretrievably as established by the defender's behaviour.[2]

  (iii) To divorce the defender from the pursuer on the ground that the marriage has broken down irretrievably as established by the defender's desertion of the pursuer for a continuous period of two years or more.[3]

  (iv) To divorce the defender from the pursuer on the ground that the marriage has broken down irretrievably as established by the parties' non-cohabitation for a continuous period of two years or more and the defender's consent to the granting of decree of divorce.[4]

  (v) To divorce the defender from the pursuer on the ground that the marriage has broken down irretrievably as established by the parties' non-cohabitation for a continuous period of five years or more.[5]

P— The marriage of the parties having broken down irretrievably, the pursuer is entitled to decree of divorce as first craved.

---

[1] 1976 Act, s.1(2)(*a*). See n. 37 *infra* and accompanying text.

[2] *Ibid.*, s.1(2)(*b*).

[3] *Ibid.*, s.1(2)(*c*).

[4] *Ibid.*, s.1(2)(*d*).

[5] *Ibid.*, s.1(2)(*e*).

2. MATRIMONIAL INTERDICT (COMMON LAW)

C—   To interdict the defender from molesting the pursuer by abusing her verbally, threatening her, putting her into a state of fear and alarm or distress or using violence towards her; and to grant interim interdict; and to attach a power of arrest to the said interim interdict.[6]

P—   The defender having molested the pursuer in the manner condescended on, and having shown an intention to persist therein, the pursuer is entitled to interdict and interim interdict as   craved.

P—   There being no circumstances to indicate that a power of arrest is unnecessary, such a power should be attached to the aforesaid interim interdict.

C—   To ordain the defender to appear personally before the court on such day and at such hour as the court may appoint to answer to the charge against him of being guilty of contempt of court and breach of the interdict granted by the Sheriff of North Strathclyde at Oban on 5 February 1995, whereby the defender was interdicted from molesting the pursuer by *inter alia* using violence towards her; and failing his appearance before the court as aforesaid, to grant warrant to officers of the court to apprehend the defender and bring him before the court to answer as aforesaid; and, on the charge being admitted or proved, to find that the defender has been guilty of contempt of court and breach of interdict and in respect thereof to visit him with such punishment as to the court shall seem just; and to find the defender liable in expenses.

P—   The defender, being in breach of interdict as

[6] The form of words is that approved in *Murdoch* v. *Murdoch*, 1973 S.L.T. (Notes) 13 for the purposes of that action. The crave's terms may be varied to suit the circumstances of the particular case, provided that it satisfies "the twin demands of competency and precision" (*Murdoch*, *supra* at p. 14). Because a power of arrest ceases to have effect upon termination of the marriage (1981 Act, s.15(2)), the crave is framed so as to seek the attachment of the power to the interim order only.

condescended on, should be found guilty and punished as craved.

3. EXCLUSION ORDER AND ANCILLARY REMEDIES

C—
(1) To grant an exclusion order suspending the defender's occupancy rights in the matrimonial home at 1 High Street, Seatown; and to grant such an order *ad interim*;

(2) To grant warrant for the summary ejection of the defender from the matrimonial home at 1 High Street, Seatown;

(3) To interdict the defender *ad interim* from entering the matrimonial home at 1 High Street, Seatown without the express permission of the pursuer; and to attach a power of arrest to the said interim interdict;

(4) To interdict the defender *ad interim* from entering or remaining in High Street, Seatown; and to attach a power of arrest to the said interim interdict; and

(5) To interdict the defender *ad interim* from removing, except with the written consent of the pursuer or by a further order of the court, any furniture or plenishings in the matrimonial home at 1 High Street, Seatown.[7]

P—
An exclusion order being in the circumstances necessary for the protection of the pursuer from reasonably apprehended conduct of the defender which would be injurious to her health, and the pursuer being entitled to the ancillary orders craved, an exclusion order suspending the defender's occupancy rights, such an order *ad interim* and orders ancillary thereto should be granted as craved.

4. PROPERTY ORDERS

C—
To find and declare that the pursuer is entitled to

---

[7] 1981 Act, s.4. In the event that part 1 of the crave is granted, part 3 must be granted by the court if the pursuer so moves (s.4(4)(*b*) and s.15(1)(*a*)); parts 2 and 5 must be granted by the court if the pursuer so moves unless the non-applicant spouse satisfies the court that it is unnecessary for them to be granted (s.4(4)(*a*) and (*c*)); the interim interdict craved in part 4 may be granted by the court (s.4(5)

occupy the dwellinghouse at 110 High Street, Seatown.[8]

P— The said dwellinghouse being a matrimonial home, the pursuer is entitled to declarator as   craved.

C— To grant leave to the pursuer to enter and occupy the matrimonial home at 110 High Street, Seatown; and to grant such leave *ad interim*.[9]

P— It being in the circumstances just and reasonable for the occupancy rights of the pursuer to be so enforced, leave to enter into and occupy the said matrimonial home should be granted as   craved.

P— It being in the circumstances necessary and expedient for the rights of the pursuer to be so enforced *ad interim*, leave to enter into and occupy the said matrimonial home should be granted *ad interim*.

C— To interdict the defender from entering the upper storey of the dwellinghouse at 110 High Street, Seatown; and to grant interim interdict.[10]

P— It being in the circumstances just and reasonable for the occupancy rights of the defender to be so restricted, interdict should be granted as   craved.

P— It being in the circumstances necessary and expedient for the rights of the defender to be so restricted *ad interim*, interim interdict should be granted.

C— To grant to the pursuer the possession and use of the items of furniture and plenishings specified in the schedule hereto in the matrimonial home at 110 High Street, Seatown; and to make such an order *ad interim*.[11]

P— It being in the circumstances just and reasonable for the pursuer to be granted the possession and use of the said

---

(*a*)), in which event the power of arrest must be attached thereto, if the pursuer so moves the court (s.15(1)(*a*)). See also nn. 46 and 47 *infra*.

[8] *Ibid.*, s.3(1)(*a*) and (3). See also nn. 46 and 47 *infra*.

[9] *Ibid.*, s.3(1)(*b*), (3) and (4). The nature and terms of the order sought depend on the circumstances of the case. See also nn. 46 and 47 *infra*.

[10] *Ibid.*, s.3(1)(*c*), (3) and (4). The nature and terms of the order sought depend on the circumstances of the case. See also nn. 46 and 47 *infra*.

[11] *Ibid.*, s.3(2), (3) and (4). See also nn. 46 and 47 *infra*.

items owned by the defender in the said matrimonial home, decree therefor should be granted as   craved.

P—   It being in the circumstances necessary and expedient for the pursuer to be granted the possession and use of the said items owned by the defender in the said matrimonial home *ad interim*, such possession and use should be granted *ad interim*.

C—   To grant decree for the transfer of the tenancy of the matrimonial home at 22 High Street, Seatown from the defender to the pursuer.[12]

P—   It being in the circumstances just and reasonable that the said tenancy should be transferred from the defender to the pursuer, decree therefor should be granted as   craved.

C—   To grant decree for the vesting of the joint tenancy of the dwellinghouse at 22 Low Street, Seatown in the pursuer solely.[13]

P—   It being in the circumstances just and reasonable that the said joint tenancy should be vested in the pursuer solely, decree should be granted as   craved.

5. CHILDREN

C—   To find the pursuer entitled to the custody of John Smith, child of the marriage and under the age of sixteen years, and Peter Jones, child of the pursuer accepted as one of the family by the defender and under the age of sixteen years.[14]

P—   It being in the best interests of the said children to be in the custody of the pursuer, the pursuer is entitled to decree therefor as   craved.

C—   To find the pursuer entitled to access to Alexander Robertson, child of the marriage and under the age of

[12] *Ibid.*, s.13 See also nn. 46 and 47 *infra*.
[13] *Ibid.* See also nn. 46 and 47 *infra*.
[14] See also nn. 40 and 43 *infra* and accompanying text regarding intimation of the action.

sixteen years, each Saturday between the hours of noon and 6 p.m.; and to residential access to him for four weeks each year during his school summer holidays and one week each year during each of his school winter and Easter holidays; or for such other period or periods as the court thinks fit.[15]

P—   It being in the best interests of the said child that the pursuer should have access to him, the pursuer is entitled to decree therefor as   craved.

C—   To ordain the defender to deliver David Davidson, child of the marriage and under the age of sixteen years, to the pursuer, and failing his doing so within such period if any as the court shall appoint, to grant warrant[16] to officers of the court to search for the said child and take possession of him and deliver him to the pursuer.

P—   The pursuer having an award of custody of the said child is entitled to decree for delivery as   craved.

C—   To grant interdict against the defender from removing James Jackson, child of the marriage and under the age of sixteen years, from Scotland or out of the control of the pursuer; and to grant such interdict *ad interim*.[17]

P—   The defender being liable to attempt to remove the said child from the control of the pursuer, interdict and interim interdict should be granted as craved.

C—   To vary the interlocutor of the Sheriff of Lothian and Borders at Edinburgh dated 15 July 1993 by awarding the pursuer custody of Elizabeth Ross, child of the parties' former marriage under the age of sixteen years.

P—   There having been a material change of circumstances and it now being in the best interests of the said child to be in the custody of the pursuer, the said interlocutor should be varied as craved.

---

[15] See also n. 43 *infra* regarding intimation of the action to the child.
[16] *Caldwell* v. *Caldwell*, 1983 S.L.T. 610.
[17] Family Law Act 1986, s.35(3).

6. MONEY

C— (i) To grant decree against the defender for payment to the pursuer of a capital sum of TEN THOUSAND POUNDS (£10,000) payable on such date and by such method as the court thinks fit with interest[18] thereon at such rate and from such date as to the court seems appropriate until payment.[19]

(ii) To grant decree for the transfer of the defender's right, title and interest in the heritable property at 4 Old Street, Avebury[20]; to ordain the defender to make, execute and deliver to the pursuer a valid disposition of the said subjects and such other deeds as may be necessary to give the pursuer a valid title to the said subjects, and that within one month of the date of decree to follow hereon; and in the event of the defender failing to make, execute and deliver such disposition and other deeds, to authorise and ordain the sheriff clerk to subscribe on behalf of the defender a disposition of the said subjects and such other deeds as may be necessary to give the pursuer a valid title to the said subjects, all as adjusted at the sight of the sheriff clerk.[21]

P— The order craved being justified by the principle set forth in s.9(1)(*a*) of the Family Law (Scotland) Act 1985 and reasonable having regard to the resources of the parties, should be granted as craved.[22]

C— (i) To grant an order for the sale of the parties' heritable property at 6 Abbey Street, Perth and for that purpose

---

[18] As to interest, see 1985 Act, s.14(2)(*j*), *Geddes* v. *Geddes*, 1993 S.L.T. 494 and other cases cited in Chap. 7, (second) n. 12.

[19] 1985 Act, s.8(1)(*a*).

[20] *Ibid.*, s.8(1)(*aa*). See Chap. 7, n. 32 regarding the description of the property sought to be transferred.

[21] The latter parts of this crave are designed to comply with observations in *Walker* v. *Walker*, 1991 S.L.T. 157; 1990 S.C.L.R. 625 (quoted in Chap. 7, n. 32). See n. 44 and accompanying text *infra* regarding intimation to a creditor where property is subject to a security.

[22] It has been suggested that the plea-in-law in support of a crave for an order for financial provision should refer to whichever of the principles in s.9(1) of the Family Law (Scotland) Act 1985 is founded upon—see *Thirde* v. *Thirde*, 1987 S.C.L.R. 335 at p. 336.

to grant warrant to such person as the court shall think proper to dispose of the said subjects, heritably and irredeemably, by public roup or private bargain, in such manner and under such conditions as the court shall direct; to ordain the pursuer and the defender to execute and deliver to the purchaser or purchasers of the said subjects such dispositions and other deeds as shall be necessary for constituting full right thereto in their persons, failing which to dispense with such execution and delivery and to direct the sheriff clerk to execute such dispositions and other deeds all as adjusted at his sight as shall be necessary aforesaid; and to make such order regarding the price of the said subjects when sold, after deduction of any debts or burdens affecting the same and all other expenses attending the sale, as to the court seems proper.[23]

(ii) To find and declare that the pursuer is the sole owner of the Ford Escort motor car, registration number K123 ABC.[24]

(iii) To grant an order entitling the pursuer to reside in the matrimonial home at 5 Low Street, Aberdeen and excluding the defender therefrom for such period following upon the granting of decree of divorce as to the court seems proper.[25]

(iv) To find the defender liable, as between the parties, for such period as to the court seems proper to make all payments due under the standard security granted by the parties in favour of the National Building Society on 5 August 1988 over the matrimonial home at 4 Princess Road, Carlops.[26]

(v) To ordain the defender to grant a standard security over his heritable property at 6 Royal Mews, Ayr in favour of the pursuer for all sums due and to become due to her in respect of the order for financial provision   craved and failing his doing so within such time as the court may specify to authorise and direct the sheriff clerk to execute such standard security, as adjusted at his sight.[27]

---

[23] *Ibid.*, s.14(2)(*a*).
[24] *Ibid.*, s.14(2)(*c*).
[25] *Ibid.*, s.14(2)(*d*).
[26] *Ibid.*, s.14(2)(*e*).
[27] *Ibid.*, s.14(2)(*f*).

(vi) To grant such other order as the court may consider appropriate.[28]

P— The order craved being appropriate in the circumstances should be granted.

C— To grant decree against the defender for payment to the pursuer of a periodical allowance of THIRTY POUNDS (£30) per week for a period of three years, or such lesser period as the court thinks fit, from the date of decree of divorce or until the death or remarriage of the pursuer, if sooner.[29]

P— The order craved being justified by the principle set forth in s.9(1)(*d*) of the Family Law (Scotland) Act 1985 and reasonable having regard to the resources of the parties and an order for payment of a capital sum or for transfer of property being insufficient *et separatim* inappropriate to satisfy the requirements of section 8(2) of the Family Law (Scotland) Act 1985, the order craved as aforesaid should be granted.

C— To grant decree against the defender for payment to the pursuer of a periodical allowance of FIFTY FIVE POUNDS (£55) per week until the death or remarriage of the pursuer or for such other lesser period as the court thinks fit.[30]

P— The order craved being justified by the principle detailed in s.9(1)(*e*) of the Family Law (Scotland) Act 1985 and reasonable having regard to the resources of the parties, and an order for payment of a capital sum or for transfer of property being insufficient *et separatim* inappropriate to satisfy the requirements of section 8(2) of the Family Law (Scotland) Act 1985, the order craved aforesaid should be granted.

[28] *Cf.* Court of Session Rule 156(2).
[29] 1985 Act, ss. 8(1)(*b*) and 13(2).
[30] *Ibid*.

C—
To interdict the defender from effecting any transfer of, or transaction involving, (1) his dwellinghouse at 1 High Street, Seatown and (2) any redundancy payment received or to be received by him from Rosebank Ltd., 15 Gold Street, Seatown, which has the effect of defeating in whole or in part the pursuer's claim for financial provision as craved; and to grant interim interdict; and to grant such other order as the court thinks fit.[31]

P—
The defender being liable to effect a transfer of, or transaction involving, his said property which is likely to have the effect of defeating the pursuer's claim for financial provision in whole or in part, interdict and interim interdict should be granted as craved.

C—
To grant an order setting aside the agreement between the parties entered into on 13 March 1992.[32]

P—
The said agreement between the parties not being fair and reasonable at the time it was entered into, should be set aside as craved.

C—
To vary the interlocutor dated 7 August 1993 insofar as providing for payment by the defender to the pursuer of a capital sum and that by substituting for the date of payment specified therein the date "7 August 1995".[33]

P—
There having been a material change of circumstances the said interlocutor should be varied as craved.

C—
To recall the order for payment of a periodical allowance by the defender to the pursuer pronounced on 15 July 1992 with effect from such date as to the court seems appropriate and to ordain the repayment by the pursuer to the defender of such sum or sums as the court thinks fit.[34]

P—
There having been a material change of circumstances the said order should be recalled as craved.

---

[31] *Ibid.*, s.18. Where there is a third party in whose favour a transfer of or transaction involving the property in question is to be or has been made, intimation is required in terms of r. 33.7(1)(*j*) (see Chap. 1, text accompanying n. 20).

[32] *Ibid.*, s.16(1)(*b*) and (2)(*b*).

[33] *Ibid.*, o.12(1).

[34] *Ibid.*, s.13(4).

7. MISCELLANEOUS

C— To grant warrant to arrest on the dependence of this action.[35]

C— To grant warrant to intimate this initial writ to Mrs Jane Jackson, residing at 2 Park Grove, Aytown, mother and one of the next of kin of the defender; and to Mamie Jackson, residing at 52 Maple Terrace, Beetown, daughter of the defender over 16 years.[36]

C— To grant warrant to intimate this initial writ to Miss Mary Black, residing at 2 Glebe Street, Seatown, as a person with whom the defender is alleged to have committed adultery.[37]

C— To grant warrant to intimate this initial writ to Mrs Indira Banda, 5 Calcutta Road, Bombay, as an additional spouse of the defender.[38]

C— To grant warrant to intimate this initial writ to Beetown District Council, Central Avenue, Beetown, as a local authority having care of the said Mark White.[39]

C— To grant warrant to intimate this initial writ to Roger Allan, residing at 1 Main Street, Beetown, as a person liable to maintain the said Peter Jones.[40]

C— To grant warrant to intimate this initial writ to Henry Smith, residing at 4 Jeffrey Street, Deetown as a person having *de facto* custody of the said Peter Smith.[41]

C— To grant warrant to intimate this initial writ to

---

[35] *Ibid.*, s.19.
[36] r. 33.7(1)(*a*) and (*c*).
[37] r. 33.7(1)(*b*).
[38] r. 33.7(1)(*d*).
[39] r. 33.7(1)(*e*)(i).
[40] r. 33.7(1)(*e*)(ii).
[41] r. 33.7(1)(*e*)(iii).

Deetown District Council, The Square, Deetown, as the local authority within which area the pursuer resides.[42]

C—   To grant warrant to intimate this initial writ to Alan Smith, 101 High Road, Efftown, as a child who is affected by this action.[43]

C—   To grant warrant to intimate this initial writ to The Huddersfield Building Society, 123 High Street, Jaytown, as holders of a security in respect of the property at 1 Johnson Terrace, Leven.[44]

C—   To grant warrant to intimate this initial writ to Peter Evans, 1 Forth Road, Dunfermline, as a person in whose favour the transfer of the property referred to in the fourth crave was made.[45].

C—   To grant warrant to intimate this initial writ to Seatown District Council, Main Square, Seatown, landlords of the matrimonial home at 1 High Street, Seatown.[46]

C—   To grant warrant to intimate this initial writ to Hugh White, residing at 4 George Place, Seatown, owner of the matrimonial home at 110 High Street, Seatown.[47]

C—   To dispense with intimation to George Banks in respect that his address is not known and cannot reasonably be ascertained.[48]

C—   To find the defender liable in expenses.

---

[42] r. 33.7(1)(*g*).

[43] r. 33.7(1)(*h*).

[44] r. 33.7(1)(*i*). See n. 21 *supra*.

[45] r. 33.7(1)(*j*). See n. 31 *supra*.

[46] r. 33.7(1)(*k*)(ii). (Intimation to landlord required where entitled spouse is tenant of the matrimonial home.)

[47] *Ibid.* (Intimation to third party required where entitled spouse is permitted to occupy the matrimonial home by third party.)

[48] r. 33.7(5).

SPECIMEN WRITS[1]
1. HUME v. HUME

A. Initial Writ
SHERIFFDOM OF NORTH STRATHCLYDE AT PAISLEY

INITIAL WRIT

in causa

MRS KATHLEEN
ALICIA ANDREWS
or HUME (Assisted
Person), residing at 331
Main Street, Paisley
PURSUER

against

EDWARD HUME,
residing
at 52 Great Queen
Street, Edinburgh
DEFENDER

The pursuer craves the court:

1. To divorce the defender from the pursuer on the ground that the marriage has broken down irretrievably as established by the defender's adultery.
2. To find the pursuer entitled to the custody of Sheila Amy Alicia Hume and George Hume, children of the marriage and under the age of 16 years.
3. To grant warrant to intimate this initial writ to Miss Racquel Smith, residing at 52 Great Queen Street, Edinburgh, as a person with whom the defender is alleged to have committed adultery.
4. To grant warrant to intimate this initial writ to Sheila Amy Alicia Hume and George Hume, both of 331 Main Street, Paisley, as children who are affected by this action.

---

[1] These are drawn from five fictitious sheriff court processes in late 1995. It should not be assumed that the styles will necessarily be acceptable in all sheriff courts.

5.   To find the defender liable in expenses.

CONDESCENDENCE

1.   The parties were married in Glasgow on 1 July 1982. They have two children: Sheila Amy Alicia Hume, born 5 July 1983, and George Hume, born 22 November 1984. Relative extract certificates of marriage and birth are produced.
2.   The pursuer has been habitually resident in Scotland throughout the period of one year immediately preceding the raising of this action. She has been resident within the Sheriffdom of North Strathclyde for a period exceeding 40 days immediately preceding the raising of this action. She is unaware of any proceedings continuing in Scotland or elsewhere which are in respect of the marriage or capable of affecting its validity or subsistence. She is unaware of any proceedings continuing or concluded in Scotland or elsewhere which relate to either of the said children.
3.   After their marriage the parties lived together until about 4 May 1993. Since then they have not lived together nor had marital relations. The defender has formed an adulterous association with Miss Racquel Smith, designed in the third crave. Since the said date they have resided together at 52 Great Queen Street, Edinburgh and have there committed adultery. On or about 7 December 1993, at said address, the defender admitted adultery to agents instructed by the pursuer. The marriage has broken down irretrievably. There is no prospect of a reconciliation. The pursuer now seeks decree of divorce.
4.   The said children reside with the pursuer. They are happy and well cared for. The pursuer is willing and able to devote her whole time and attention to them and provide them with a good home. It is in the best interests of the said children to be in the custody of the pursuer.

PLEAS-IN-LAW

1.   The marriage of the parties having broken down irretrievably, the pursuer is entitled to decree of divorce as first craved.
2.   It being in the best interests of the said children to be in the custody of the pursuer, the pursuer is entitled to decree therefor as second craved.

IN RESPECT
WHEREOF

Enrolled Solicitor
503 Bank Street
Paisley
Solicitor for Pursuer

2. SMART v. SMART

A. Initial Writ, including Minute for Decree
SHERIFFDOM OF GLASGOW AND STRATHKELVIN AT
GLASGOW

INITIAL WRIT

in causa

JOANNA WYSE or
SMART (Assisted
Person), residing at 4
Gardeners Crescent,
Springboig, Glasgow
PURSUER

against

HENRY JOSEPH
SMART,
residing at 14 Grove
Place, Dennistoun,
Glasgow
DEFENDER

The pursuer craves the court:
1. To divorce the defender from the pursuer on the ground that the marriage has broken down irretrievably as established by the defender's behaviour.
2. To interdict the defender from molesting the pursuer by abusing her verbally, threatening her, putting her into a state of fear and alarm or distress or using violence towards her; and to grant interim interdict; and to attach a power of arrest to the said interim interdict.
3. To find the defender liable in expenses.

CONDESCENDENCE

1. The parties were married at Glasgow on 20 November 1991. They have no children. Extract certificate of marriage is produced.
2. The pursuer was born in Scotland and has lived in Scotland all her life. She intends to remain permanently resident in Scotland. She is domiciled in Scotland. She has been resident in the Sheriffdom of Glasgow and Strathkelvin for a period exceeding 40 days immediately preceding the raising of this action. She knows of no proceedings continuing in Scotland or elsewhere which are in

respect of the marriage or capable of affecting its validity or
subsistence.

3. The marriage has broken down irretrievably as established by the
    defender's behaviour. He developed an alcohol problem. Latterly he
    drank every day. He would regularly return home drunk late at
    night. He would become heavily intoxicated at social events to the
    embarrassment and humiliation of the pursuer. He spent little time
    at home. He did little to assist in the management of the household.
    The defender's said behaviour adversely affected the pursuer's
    health. On or about 6 June 1994, the parties separated. Since then they
    have not lived together nor had marital relations. The pursuer cannot
    reasonably be expected to cohabit with the defender. There is no
    prospect of a reconciliation. The pursuer now seeks decree of
    divorce.

4. Following the parties' separation aforesaid the defender has
    persistently molested the pursuer. He has frequently abused her by
    telephone. He has threatened to assault her if she does not resume
    cohabitation with him. He has followed her in the street demanding a
    reconciliation. In particular, on or about 5 August 1994, the defender
    shouted abuse and threats at the pursuer from the street outside her
    house. The pursuer is apprehensive that he will continue so to act.
    She is fearful lest he carry out the said threats. She accordingly seeks
    the protection of the interdict, interim interdict and power of arrest
    second craved.

PLEAS-IN-LAW

1. The marriage of the parties having broken down irretrievably, the
    pursuer is entitled to decree of divorce as first craved.
2. The defender having molested the pursuer in the manner
    condescended on, and having shown an intention to persist therein,
    the pursuer is entitled to interdict and interim interdict as second
    craved.
3. There being no circumstances to indicate that a power of arrest is
    unnecessary, such a power should be attached to the aforesaid
    interim interdict.

IN RESPECT
WHEREOF

Enrolled Solicitor
692 West George
Street
Glasgow
Solicitor for Pursuer

WADDELL having considered the evidence contained in the affidavits
and the other documents all as specified in the schedule hereto and

being satisfied that upon the evidence a motion for decree in terms of the first and third craves of the initial writ may properly be made, moves the court accordingly.

IN RESPECT
WHEREOF

Solicitor for Pursuer

SCHEDULE

1. Affidavit of pursuer.
2. Affidavit of Glenda Parkes or Wilson.
3. Marriage certificate no. 2/1 of process.

B. Affidavit of Pursuer

SHERIFFDOM OF GLASGOW AND STRATHKELVIN AT
GLASGOW

AFFIDAVIT

of Pursuer

in causa

JOANNA WYSE or
SMART (Assisted
Person), residing at
4 Gardeners Crescent,
Springboig, Glasgow
PURSUER

against

HENRY JOSEPH
SMART, residing at
14 Grove Place,
Dennistoun, Glasgow
DEFENDER

At Glasgow, the Fifteenth day of December Nineteen Hundred and Ninety Four, in the presence of ALLAN WADDELL, Solicitor and Notary Public, 692 West George Street, Glasgow, Compeared: JOANNA WYSE or SMART, residing at 4 Gardeners Crescent, Springboig, Glasgow, who being solemnly sworn, Depones as follows:
1.   My full name is Joanna Wyse or Smart. I am 25 years of age, a part-

time teller in Citibank, and I reside at 4 Gardeners Crescent, Springboig, Glasgow.

2. I married my husband, Henry Joseph Smart, at present residing at 14 Grove Place, Dennistoun, Glasgow, at Glasgow on 20 November 1991. We have no children. I produce an extract of the entry in the Register of Marriages, no. 2/1 of process, which I have signed as relative hereto.

3. I was born in Scotland and have lived here all my life and intend to continue doing so. I was resident in the Sheriffdom of Glasgow and Strathkelvin for at least forty days prior to raising this action of divorce. I do not know of any proceedings continuing in Scotland or elsewhere concerning my marriage or capable of affecting its validity or subsistence.

4. My marriage has broken down irretrievably. I believe that my husband had a drinking problem when we got married but it became progressively worse. Eventually he would never come home without calling in at the pub on the way. When he returned home, he would stay for a short time only before going back out to the pub, where he would stay drinking until closing time. He would then come home drunk. He worked as a TV engineer with Johnsons of Edinburgh Road, Glasgow until he was sacked on account of his drinking.

My husband's drinking caused me humiliation and embarrassment at the few social events that we attended. My husband behaved so badly at these, because he was hopelessly drunk, that I had to spend almost the entire evening apologising. On one particular occasion, at a disco for a charity held after the death of a friend of mine, I felt particularly bad because my husband had been rude and unpleasant to everybody and had embarrassed and humiliated me in front of a good number of my friends.

My husband also did virtually nothing to assist with running the house, although I cannot say that he kept me short of money. It was only grudgingly that he ever helped in the decoration of our home, and apart from that he never did anything at all, not even drying the dishes.

Although my husband never assaulted me, his behaviour certainly affected my health and nerves. I would often get asthmatic attacks because of the stress I felt. Eventually, I felt that I could no longer tolerate his behaviour. On 6 June, 1994, I left him and we have neither lived together nor had marital relations since.

Following our separation my husband pestered me by telephone and in the streets, making various threats to hurt me if I did not go back to him. Since I obtained a court order against him to stop him molesting me, I have heard nothing more from him. I confirm that there is no prospect of a reconciliation between us.

All of which is truth as the deponent shall answer to God.

.... Deponent

...... Notary Public

C. Affidavit of Glenda Parkes or Wilson
SHERIFFDOM OF GLASGOW AND STRATHKELVIN AT
GLASGOW

AFFIDAVIT

of Mrs Glenda Parkes
or Wilson

in causa

JOANNA WYSE or
SMART (Assisted
Person), residing at
4 Gardeners Crescent,
Springboig, Glasgow
PURSUER

against

HENRY JOSEPH
SMART, residing at
14 Grove Place,
Dennistoun, Glasgow
DEFENDER

At Glasgow, the Fifteenth day of December Nineteen Hundred and
Ninety Four, in the presence of ALLAN WADDELL, Solicitor and Notary
Public, 692 West George Street, Glasgow, Compeared GLENDA
PARKES or WILSON, residing at 43 Queen's Road, Springboig, Glasgow,
who being solemnly sworn, Depones as follows:
1. My full name is Glenda Parkes or Wilson. I am 27 years of age, a part-
    time sales assistant and reside at 43 Queen's Road, Springboig,
    Glasgow.
2. I have been a friend of Joanna Smart, the pursuer in this action, for
    several years. I came to know her husband pretty well and am able to
    speak to events during their marriage from my own personal
    knowledge. I am aware that Mrs Smart and her husband have been
    separated since about June of this year. I also know why their
    relationship broke down: it was solely as a result of the defender's
    increasing addiction to drink. He seemed to drink virtually every
    day. He often came round to my house to try to persuade my
    husband to go drinking with him. Usually he had already had a few
    and was quite drunk.
    I would say that there was a definite effect on Mrs Smart's health.
    She has asthma and his behaviour affected her asthmatic condition.
    Before the separation she had to use her inhaler far more often than

ever before. There were days also when I went to her house and found her sitting in the kitchen in floods of tears. The whole marital relationship slid to rock-bottom as a result of his drinking and its effect on her. I have been at a number of social occasions which they attended before they separated at which he was drunk and I know that she was embarrassed by his behaviour at them. I do not see them ever getting back together again.

All of which is truth as the deponent shall answer to God.

.... Deponent

...... Notary Public

3. SCOTT v. SCOTT

A. Initial Writ

SHERIFFDOM OF LOTHIAN AND BORDERS AT EDINBURGH

INITIAL WRIT

in causa

MRS ANN
GEORGE
or SCOTT
(Assisted Person),
residing at
5 Merton Grove,
Edinburgh
PURSUER

against

PHILIP SCOTT,
residing at 14
Elm Grove,
Dalkeith
DEFENDER

The pursuer craves the court:
1. To divorce the defender from the pursuer on the ground that the marriage has broken down irretrievably as established by the defender's desertion of the pursuer for a continuous period of two years or more.
2. To find the pursuer entitled to the custody of Daphne Scott, child of

the marriage and under the age of 16 years, which failing, to find the pursuer entitled to access to the said child each weekend between the hours of 6 p.m. on Friday and 6 p.m. on Sunday; or for such other period or periods as the court thinks fit.

3. To grant warrant to intimate this initial writ to Mrs Elspeth Scott, residing at 22 George Place, Dalkeith as a person having *de facto* custody of the said Daphne Scott.
4. To grant warrant to intimate this initial writ to Daphne Scott, 22 George Place, Dalkeith, as a child who is affected by this action.
5. To find the defender liable in expenses.

CONDESCENDENCE

1. The parties were married at Edinburgh on 1 March 1983. They have one child, Daphne Scott born 25 June 1984. Relative extract certificates of marriage and birth are produced.
2. The pursuer was born in Scotland of Scottish parents and has lived most of her life in Scotland. She intends to reside permanently in Scotland. She is domiciled in Scotland. She has been resident within the Sheriffdom of Lothian and Borders for a period exceeding 40 days immediately preceding the raising of this action. She is unaware of any proceedings continuing in Scotland or elsewhere which are in respect of the marriage or capable of affecting its validity or subsistence. She is unaware of any proceedings continuing or concluded in Scotland or elsewhere which relate to the said child.
3. After the marriage the parties lived together until about June 1991, when the defender deserted the pursuer. The pursuer was then willing to adhere. The defender had no reasonable cause so to act. Since then the parties have not lived together nor had marital relations. The pursuer has not refused a genuine and reasonable offer by the defender to adhere. The marriage has broken down irretrievably. There is no prospect of a reconciliation. The pursuer now seeks decree of divorce.
4. After the parties' separation, the child resided with the pursuer. On or about 4 March 1994, at or about 7 p.m. the defender came to the pursuer's house. He demanded immediate access to the said child. The pursuer declined to accede. The defender thereupon assaulted her. He forcibly entered the said house and seized the child. He removed the child to the house of his mother, Mrs Elspeth Scott, designed in the third crave. The child remains in the *de facto* custody of Mrs Scott. It is not in the best interests of the child to reside with the said Mrs Scott or with the defender. The child was well settled and happy with the pursuer. She attended the local school where she performed well. The child wishes to reside with the pursuer. It is in her best interests to be in the custody of the pursuer, which failing for the pursuer to have access as second craved.

PLEAS-IN-LAW

1. The marriage of the parties having broken down irretrievably, the pursuer is entitled to decree of divorce as first craved.
2. It being in the best interests of the child to be in the custody of the pursuer, failing which for the pursuer to have access and interim access to her, the pursuer is entitled to decree therefor as second craved.

IN RESPECT
WHEREOF

Enrolled Solicitor
42 St. Charlotte
Street
Edinburgh
Solicitor for Pursuer

B. Defences

SHERIFFDOM OF LOTHIAN AND BORDERS AT EDINBURGH

DEFENCES

in causa

MRS ANN
GEORGE
or SCOTT
(Assisted Person),
residing at 5
Merton Grove,
Edinburgh
                    PURSUER

against

PHILIP SCOTT,
residing at 14
Elm Grove,
Dalkeith
                    DEFENDER

The defender craves the court:
To find the defender entitled to the custody of Daphne Scott, child of the marriage and under the age of 16 years.

ANSWERS TO CONDESCENDENCE

1. Admitted under explanation that the defender now resides at 22 George Place, Dalkeith.
2. Believed to be true. The defender knows of no such proceedings.
3. No admission is made.
4. Admitted that after the parties' separation the child resided with the pursuer. Admitted that on 4 March 1994 at about 7 p.m. the defender came to the pursuer's house. Admitted that he requested access to the child. Admitted that he removed the said child to the house of his mother, Mrs Elspeth Scott. Admitted that the child attended the local school. Not known and not admitted how she performed there. *Quoad ultra* denied. Explained and averred that on 4 March 1994 at about 7 p.m. the defender called at the pursuer's house. He requested access to the child. The pursuer thrust the child into the defender's arms. She told him to keep her for good. The pursuer was drunk at the time. The defender believes and avers that the pursuer is frequently under the influence of alcohol. Her house is dirty. The child was not being properly looked after. Her clothing was torn and filthy. She required to be thoroughly scrubbed at the defender's mother's house where she now resides. There is ample accommodation for her. She is well looked after by both the defender and his said mother. She is happy living with them. She is settling well at her new school. It is in her best interests to be in the custody of the defender. The defender believes and avers that it is further in the best interests of the child for the pursuer to have non-residential access only to her.

PLEAS-IN-LAW

1. It not being in the best interests of the child to be in the custody of the pursuer nor for the pursuer to have residential access to her, decree therefor should not be pronounced as craved.
2. It being in the best interests of the child to be in the custody of the defender, decree therefor should be pronounced as craved.

IN RESPECT
WHEREOF

Enrolled Solicitor
4 Market Street
Dalkeith
Solicitor for
Defender

4. JAMIESON v. JAMIESON

A. Initial Writ, including Minute for Decree

SHERIFFDOM OF GRAMPIAN, HIGHLAND AND ISLANDS AT
STONEHAVEN

INITIAL WRIT

in causa

ROBERT JAMIESON,
residing at 4 Dundas
Street, Stonehaven
PURSUER

against

MRS OLIVE HANSON
or ROBERTSON or
JAMIESON, residing at
4 Nursery Street,
Stonehaven
DEFENDER

The pursuer craves the court:
1. To divorce the defender from the pursuer on the ground that the marriage has broken down irretrievably as established by the parties' non-cohabitation for a continuous period of two years or more and the defender's consent to the granting of decree of divorce.
2. To grant warrant to intimate this initial writ to Hamish Wilson Robertson, residing at 1 Forge Park, Brechin, Angus as a person who is liable to maintain Peter Robertson, residing at 4 Nursery Street, Stonehaven.
3. To grant warrant to intimate this initial writ to Peter Robertson, residing at 4 Nursery Street, Stonehaven, as a child who is affected by this action.

CONDESCENDENCE

1. The parties were married at Edinburgh on 5 December 1990. They have no children. The defender has a child accepted as one of the family by the pursuer: Peter Robertson, born 5 July 1988. Extract certificates of marriage and birth are produced. The natural father of the said Peter Robertson is Hamish Wilson Robertson, designed in the second crave.
2. The pursuer has been habitually resident in Scotland throughout the

period of one year immediately preceding the raising of this action. He has been resident within the Sheriffdom of Grampian, Highland and Islands for a period exceeding 40 days immediately preceding the raising of this action. He is unaware of any proceedings continuing in Scotland or elsewhere which are in respect of the marriage or capable of affecting its validity or subsistence.

3. After their marriage the parties lived together until about January 1992. Since then they have not lived together nor had marital relations. The defender is prepared to consent to the granting of decree of divorce. The marriage has broken down irretrievably. There is no prospect of a reconciliation. The pursuer seeks decree of divorce.

4. The said child resides with the defender and is well looked after. The present arrangements for his care and upbringing are satisfactory.

PLEA-IN-LAW

The marriage of the parties having broken down irretrievably, the pursuer is entitled to decree of divorce as first craved.

IN RESPECT
WHEREOF

Enrolled Solicitor
10 Main Square
Stonehaven
Solicitor for Pursuer

UNMAN having considered the evidence contained in the affidavits and the other documents all as specified in the schedule hereto and being satisfied that upon the evidence a motion for decree in terms of the first crave of the initial writ may properly be made, moves the court accordingly.

IN RESPECT
WHEREOF

Solicitor for Pursuer

SCHEDULE

1. Affidavit of pursuer.
2. Affidavit of defender.
3. Affidavit of Mrs Jeannie Hogg or Hanson.
4. Marriage certificate, no. 2/1 of process.
5. Birth certificate, no. 2/2 of process.
6. Notice of Consent, no. 2/3 of process.

B. Affidavit of Pursuer

SHERIFFDOM OF GRAMPIAN, HIGHLAND AND ISLANDS AT STONEHAVEN

AFFIDAVIT

of pursuer

in causa

ROBERT JAMIESON,
residing at 4 Dundas
Street, Stonehaven
PURSUER

against

MRS OLIVE HANSON
or ROBERTSON or
JAMIESON, residing at
4 Nursery Street,
Stonehaven
DEFENDER

At Stonehaven, the Seventh day of September Nineteen Hundred and Ninety Four, in the presence of JOHN UNMAN, Notary Public, 10 Main Square, Stonehaven, Compeared: ROBERT JAMIESON, residing at 4 Dundas Street, Stonehaven, who being solemnly sworn, Depones as follows:

1. My full name is Robert Jamieson. I am aged 42 years and I reside at 4 Dundas Street, Stonehaven. I am unemployed.
2. I was married to Olive Hanson or Robertson or Jamieson, presently residing at 4 Nursery Street, Stonehaven at Edinburgh on 5 December 1990. We have no children. My wife has a child from a previous marriage: Peter Robertson, born 5 July 1988 whose natural father is Hamish Wilson Robertson, residing at 1 Forge Park, Brechin, Angus. I accepted Peter Robertson as one of the family. I produce extracts of the relevant entries in the Registers of Marriages and Births, numbers 2/1 and 2/2 of process, which I have docqueted as relative hereto.
3. I have been habitually resident in Scotland throughout the period of one year immediately preceding the raising of this action. I have been resident within the Sheriffdom of Grampian, Highland and Islands for a period exceeding 40 days immediately preceding the raising of this action. I am not aware of any proceedings continuing in Scotland or elsewhere which are in respect of the marriage or capable of affecting its validity or subsistence.

4. After the marriage my wife and I lived together until about January 1992. Since then we have not lived together nor had marital relations. There is no prospect of a reconciliation. My wife consents to the granting of decree of divorce. I identify her signature on the Form of Consent, no. 2/3 of process, which I have docqueted as relative hereto.

5. Since the separation I have seen very little of the child, Peter. I am not in a position to speak to the present arrangements for his care and upbringing.

   All of which is truth as the Deponent shall answer to God.

   .... Deponent

   .... Notary Public

C. Affidavit of Oliver Jamieson

SHERIFFDOM OF GRAMPIAN, HIGHLAND AND ISLANDS AT STONEHAVEN

AFFIDAVIT

of Oliver Jamieson

in causa

ROBERT JAMIESON,
residing at 4 Dundas
Street, Stonehaven
PURSUER

against

MRS OLIVE HANSON
or ROBERTSON or
JAMIESON, residing
at 4 Nursery Street,
Stonehaven
DEFENDER

At Stonehaven, the Seventh day of September Nineteen Hundred and Ninety Four, in the presence of JOHN UNMAN, Notary Public, 10 Main Square, Stonehaven, Compeared: Oliver Jamieson, residing at 4 Dundas Street, Stonehaven, who being solemnly sworn, Depones as follows:

1. My full name is Oliver Jamieson. I am aged 67 years. I reside at 4 Dundas Street, Stonehaven. I am retired. I am the father of Robert Jamieson, the pursuer in this action.

2. My son lives with me. I am aware that he separated from his wife in

January 1992. He did in fact come to stay with me at that time and has lived with me ever since, I therefore know that he has not lived as man and wife with her since then.

All of which is truth as the Deponent shall answer to God.

.... Deponent

.... Notary Public

D. Affidavit of Defender

SHERIFFDOM OF GRAMPIAN, HIGHLAND AND ISLANDS AT STONEHAVEN

AFFIDAVIT

of defender

in causa

ROBERT JAMIESON,
residing at 4 Dundas
Street, Stonehaven
        PURSUER

against

MRS OLIVE HANSON
or ROBERTSON or
JAMIESON, residing
at 4 Nursery Street,
Stonehaven
        DEFENDER

At Stonehaven, the Twenty First day of September Nineteen Hundred and Ninety Four, in the presence of ALAN MARSH, Notary Public, 11 New Street, Stonehaven, Compeared: MRS OLIVE HANSON or ROBERTSON or JAMIESON, residing at 4 Nursery Street, Stonehaven, who being solemnly sworn, Depones as follows:

1. My full name is Olive Hanson or Robertson or Jamieson. I am aged 32 years and reside at 4 Nursery Street, Stonehaven. I am a housewife.
2. My son Peter Robertson has lived with me since my separation from my husband. Although Peter was a bit upset at the break-up of our marriage, he has come on well since. He stays with me in the former matrimonial home at 4 Nursery Street, Stonehaven. The house is a Scottish Homes house and is well furnished. It comprises a livingroom, two bedrooms, livingroom/kitchenette and bathroom. Peter has one bedroom and I have the other. Peter attends St. Mark's

Primary School near my house and is getting on well there. He has lots of friends with whom he plays regularly. I do not work an devote my whole time and attention to Peter's care and wellbeing. He is a happy and healthy boy. Peter has little contact with my husband and does not seem to miss him now.

All of which is truth as the Deponent shall answer to God.

.... Deponent

.... Notary Public

E. Affidavit of Mrs Jeannie Hogg or Hanson

SHERIFFDOM OF GRAMPIAN, HIGHLAND AND ISLANDS AT STONEHAVEN

AFFIDAVIT

of Mrs Jeannie Hogg or Hanson

in causa

ROBERT JAMIESON, residing at 4 Dundas Street, Stonehaven
PURSUER

against

MRS OLIVE HANSON or ROBERTSON or JAMIESON, residing at 4 Nursery Street, Stonehaven
DEFENDER

At Stonehaven the Twenty First day of September Nineteen Hundred and Ninety Four in the presence of ALAN MARSH, Notary Public, 11 New Street, Stonehaven, Compeared: MRS JEANNIE HOGG or HANSON, residing at 66 Nursery Street, Stonehaven, who being solemnly sworn, Depones as follows:

1. My full name is Jeannie Hogg or Hanson. I am 55 years of age and reside at 66 Nursery Street, Stonehaven. I am a housewife. I am the mother of the defender, Mrs Olive Hanson or Robertson or Jamieson.

2. I remember my daughter and her husband separating in about January 1992. Since then my grandson Peter has lived with my daughter in the former matrimonial home at 4 Nursery Street,

Stonehaven. My daughter does not work and devotes all her time to looking after Peter. He is always healthy and happy. Although he was upset when my son-in-law left the family home, he seems to be over it now and rarely sees my son-in-law now. My daughter and Peter live in a Scottish Homes house which has a livingroom, livingroom/kitchenette, two bedrooms and bathroom. Peter has his own bedroom; my daughter has the other. Peter now attends St. Mark's Primary School, Stonehaven and I know he enjoys it. He is forever off to play with some new friend or other. He really loves his mother.

All of which is truth as the Deponent shall answer to God.

.... Deponent

.... Notary Public

A. Initial Writ

SHERIFFDOM OF SOUTH STRATHCLYDE, DUMFRIES AND
GALLOWAY AT STRANRAER

INITIAL WRIT

in causa

JOHN BANKS,
residing at 3 Almond
Place, Stranraer
                    PURSUER

against

MRS ANNIE
ALLISON or BANKS,
his wife, residing at 1
Park Street, Peebles
                    DEFENDER

The pursuer craves the court:
1. To divorce the defender from the pursuer on the ground that the marriage has broken down irretrievably as established by the parties' non-cohabitation for a continuous period of five years or more.
2. To grant warrant to intimate this initial writ to Strathclyde Regional Council, Strathclyde House, 20 India Street, Glasgow, as a local authority having care of Peter Banks, child of the marriage and under the age of 16 years.

3. To grant warrant to intimate this initial writ to Peter Banks, ^c/o Strathclyde Regional Council, Strathclyde House, 20 India Street, Glasgow, as a child who is affected by this action.

CONDESCENDENCE

1. The parties were married at Hamilton on 5 June 1967. There is one child of the marriage under the age of 16 years: Peter Banks, born 5 June 1979. Relative extract certificates of marriage and birth are produced.
2. The defender has been habitually resident in Scotland throughout the period of one year immediately preceding the raising of this action. The pursuer has been resident within the Sheriffdom of South Strathclyde, Dumfries and Galloway for a period exceeding 40 days immediately preceding the raising of this action. He is unaware of any proceedings continuing in Scotland or elsewhere which are in respect of the marriage or capable of affecting its validity or subsistence.
3. After their marriage the parties lived together until about January 1989. Since then they have not lived together nor had marital relations. The marriage has broken down irretrievably. There is no prospect of a reconciliation. The pursuer seeks decree of divorce.
4. The said child is at present in the care of Strathclyde Regional Council, designed in the second crave.
5. The pursuer is employed as a labourer and earns about £220 per week. He has savings of about £2,000. He has no other capital. He aliments the defender at the rate of £50 per week in terms of an order by the Sheriff at Peebles dated 4 March 1992. He is otherwise unaware of the defender's present financial circumstances.

PLEA-IN-LAW

The marriage of the parties having broken down irretrievably, the pursuer is entitled to decree of divorce as first craved.

IN RESPECT
WHEREOF

Enrolled Solicitor
1 Fleet Street
Stranraer
Solicitor for Pursuer

SHERIFFDOM OF SOUTH STRATHCLYDE, DUMFRIES AND
GALLOWAY AT STRANRAER

DEFENCES

in causa

JOHN BANKS,
residing at 4 Almond
Place, Stranraer
PURSUER

against

MRS ANNIE
ALLISON or BANKS,
residing at 1 Park
Street, Peebles
DEFENDER

The defender craves the court:
1. To grant decree against the pursuer for payment to the defender of a capital sum of ONE THOUSAND POUNDS (£1,000), payable at such date and by such method as the court thinks fit, with interest on such proportion thereof at such rate and from such date as the court thinks fit until payment.
2. To grant decree against the pursuer for payment to the defender of a periodical allowance of SIXTY FIVE POUNDS (£65) per week for a period of three years, or such lesser period as the court thinks fit, from the date of decree of divorce or until the death or remarriage of the defender, if sooner.

ANSWERS TO CONDESCENDENCE

1. Admitted.
2. Admitted. The defender knows of no such proceedings.
3. Admitted.
4. Admitted.
5. The averment anent the maintenance order is admitted. *Quoad ultra* not known and not admitted. Explained and averred that the defender is aged 52 years. She keeps reasonable health. She has no qualifications. She is in employment as a clerkess and earns about £120 per week. She has been dependent on the pursuer for financial support throughout the marriage. She has enjoyed a reasonably comfortable standard of living. She has no capital. She made a substantial contribution to the marriage. She looked after the family home and cared for the pursuer and the parties' five children. In all the circumstances, the pursuer is entitled to a fair sharing

of the matrimonial property and an order enabling her to adjust to the loss of financial support. Decree should be granted as first and second craved.

1. The order first craved being justified by the principle set forth in s.9(1)(*a*) of the Family Law (Scotland) Act 1985 and reasonable having regard to the parties' resources should be granted.
2. The order second craved being justified by the principle set forth in s.9(1)(*d*) of the Family Law (Scotland) Act 1985 and reasonable having regard to the parties' resources and an order for payment of a capital sum being insufficient to satisfy the requirements of section 8(2) of the Act, the order second craved should be granted.

IN RESPECT
WHEREOF

Enrolled Solicitor
42 Ainslie Street
Ayr
Solicitor for Defender

C. Joint Minute for Parties

SHERIFFDOM OF SOUTH STRATHCLYDE, DUMFRIES AND
GALLOWAY AT STRANRAER

JOINT MINUTE

for the parties

in causa

JOHN BANKS residing
at 4 Almond Place,
Stranraer
    PURSUER

against

MRS ANNIE
ALLISON or BANKS,
residing at 1 Park
Street, Peebles
    DEFENDER

JONES for the pursuer and

ZIGO for the defender concurred and hereby concur in stating to the court that in the event of decree of divorce being granted and subject to the approval of the court the parties have agreed and hereby agree as follows:

1. The pursuer shall pay to the defender a capital sum of NINE HUNDRED POUNDS (£900), payable upon the granting of decree of divorce, with interest thereon at the rate of eight *per centum per annum* from the date of decree to follow hereon until payment; and

2. The pursuer shall pay to the defender a periodical allowance of SIXTY POUNDS (£60) per week for a period of two years from the date of decree of divorce or until the death or remarriage of the defender, if sooner.

The parties therefore craved and hereby crave the court to interpone authority hereto and grant decree in terms hereof.

IN RESPECT
WHEREOF

Enrolled Solicitor
1 Fleet Street
Stranraer
Solicitor for Pursuer

Enrolled Solicitor
42 Ainslie Street
Ayr
Solicitor for Defender

COURT PRACTICE RE DIVORCE AFFIDAVITS[1]

1. An affidavit is no substitute for a reliable and adequate precognition, though a precognition may eventually be the basis for an affidavit.

2. The affidavit should be typed on substantial paper, should be backed up longways, and should be stitched or stapled. It must commence with the words "At   , the   day of   19   , in the presence of   Compeared   who being solemnly sworn, Depones as follows   ,". The full name, age, address and occupation must be given, and it must thereafter proceed in the first person and should take the form of numbered paragraphs. The witness should be made to appreciate the importance of the affidavit. The witness must be placed on oath, or must affirm, and each page will require to be signed by both the witness and the notary. It is not essential that it should be sealed by the notary. The document should be of a shape and size convenient to be lodged as part of the process. The affidavit should end with the words, "All of which is truth as the deponent shall answer to God," or "All of which is affirmed to be true," as appropriate.

3. Affidavits of parties and witnesses should follow step-by-step the averments in the initial writ. The drafter of an affidavit should provide himself, before drawing it, with a copy of the initial writ, a copy of the appropriate precognition, and the relative productions. The affidavit to be taken from a witness should follow the averments in the initial writ to the extent that these are within the knowledge of that particular witness. It is not a requirement that the wording of an affidavit should follow exactly the wording of the initial writ.

4. [*No hearsay.*] The drafter must take care that an affidavit [contains only matters of fact to which the party or the witness in

---

[1] Appendix III comprises the terms of the Acts of Court or Practice Notes of all the sheriffdoms relative to affidavits in undefended actions of divorce, with local variations as indicated.

question can testify, and that it] is correct at the date at which it is sworn).[2]

5. On the matter of the qualifications of the person before whom the affidavit is taken, the Rules provide that the affidavit is admissible if it is duly emitted before a notary public or other competent authority. This means a notary public, justice of the peace, commissioner of oaths or other statutory authority within the meaning of the Statutory Declarations Act 1835. In the examples given hereafter, it is assumed that the affidavit is in fact taken before a solicitor who is a notary public, and therefore the references to the party before whom the affidavit is sworn are to "the notary." The solicitor acting in the action may well be called on also to act in a notarial capacity when the affidavit is subsequently sworn. This is permissible. In acting in a notarial capacity he must, however, as a competent authority, observe all the normal rules in this connection, and must satisfy himself as to the capacity of the witness to make the statement, and ensure that the witness understands that it constitutes his or her evidence in the case.

6. On the matter of productions, those required, when an affidavit is being taken, may already have been lodged in process, but there may be some productions (such as photographs) which are produced by the witness to the notary when the affidavit is sworn, and which may not by that time have been lodged in process.

7. Productions already lodged in process must be borrowed up, and put to the party or the witness who makes them part of his evidence in the appropriate part of the affidavit. Each production will require to be referred to in the affidavit by its number of process and must be docqueted and signed by the party or witness and the notary. If a production has not yet been lodged when the affidavit is being taken, it will require to be identified by the witness in his evidence in the affidavit, and will then be docqueted with regard to the affidavit and signed by the party or witness and the notary. It will then be lodged as a production. Obviously, certain productions will be docqueted with regard to more than one affidavit.

8. In adultery cases, photographs of both the pursuer and the

---

[2] Words in square brackets deleted by Practice Note, June 1991, by the Sheriff Principal of Glasgow and Strathkelvin; and the whole paragraph omitted from the Sheriffdom of Lothian and Borders Act of Court (Consolidation, etc.) 1990 No. 1.

defender will require to be produced, put to the appropriate party or witnesses in the affidavit, and signed and docqueted with reference thereto in the manner already described. [In certain circumstances, a photograph may have to be identified and docqueted by more than one person, as in the case of the photograph of a party requiring to be spoken to by the pursuer and two inquiry agents.][3]

9. All affidavits lodged must be of as recent a date as is possible in the circumstances. This factor is particularly important in (1) cases involving children, (2) those in which financial craves are involved, or (3) in any other circumstances where the evidence of a party or witness is liable to change through the passage of time. The notary will require to ensure, therefore, that an affidavit represents the deponent's evidence on such matters at the time the affidavit is sworn.

10. In cases involving custody of or access to children, an affidavit or affidavits providing corroborating evidence about the welfare of the children should be provided. The evidence of that witness must present the court with a full picture of the position regarding the child or children. It is, however, clear that such independent evidence in no way relieves the pursuer from testifying fully the position regarding the children in his or her own affidavit, so far as within his or her knowledge. Whatever else the affidavits of the pursuer and the independent witness contain, their evidence should certainly include the following:

(a) the qualifications of the witness, if not a parent, to speak about the child; how often, for example, and in what circumstances, does the witness normally see the child;

(b) a description of the home conditions in which the child lives;

(c) observations upon the child's general appearance, interests, state of health and well-being;

(d) information, where relevant, about the school the child attends; whether and to what extent he has contact with other children and relatives;

(e) observations on the relationship between the child and the person in whose care he or she lives, on the child's attitude towards each of the parents and on

---

[3] Words in square brackets deleted by Practice Note, June 1991, by the Sheriff Principal of Glasgow and Strathkelvin and omitted from the Sheriffdom of North Strathclyde Act of Court (Consolidation, etc.) 1992.

the extent of contact with the parent or parents with whom the child is not living;

(f) details of child care arrangements at all times including arrangements during working hours (outwith school hours);

(g) the means and status of the person craving custody with a view to enabling him or her to maintain and bring up the child in a suitable manner.

11. The attention of solicitors is drawn to the provisions of the Matrimonial Proceedings (Children) Act 1958. The court will not (unless the provisions of section 8(2) are shown to apply) grant decree of divorce until the court is satisfied, as respects every child for whose custody, maintenance and education the court has jurisdiction to make provision in that action, (a) that arrangements have been made for the care and upbringing of the child and that those arrangements are satisfactory or are the best which can be devised in the circumstances; or (b) that it is impracticable for the party or parties appearing before the court to make any such arrangements.

12. Where financial conclusions are involved, it is even more important that the evidence is full, accurate and up-to-date. In parole proofs the evidence of the pursuer and the witnesses on these matters can be supplemented at the proof by questions from the bench or from the solicitor for the pursuer. This will not be possible where evidence is taken by affidavit, and the affidavits must be so framed as to exclude the necessity for supplementary questions. Failure to do so may result in the sheriff requiring the attendance of the solicitor in court. If, after an affidavit has been taken, and the solicitor concerned has parted with it, a material change of circumstances occurs, it is essential that the court be immediately informed, and where necessary, that a further affidavit be sworn.

13. Where the pursuer in an action is speaking in the affidavit of the financial position of the defender, it is essential that the affidavit should state the date, as precisely as possible, at which that information was valid. Otherwise it may be assumed by the court that the pursuer is speaking to the defender's position at the date of the affidavit. The court must be provided with as up-to-date information as possible about the defender's ability to pay the sums the pursuer is seeking, and these sums should be such as that evidence justifies. The pursuer must, of course, speak also to his or her own financial position, at the date of the affidavit. Where the pursuer cannot obtain recent information as to the defender's means, it is suggested that, if the pursuer's advisers

approve, assessment should be left to the sheriff, and in such cases it may be that the solicitors representing the pursuer would be willing to incorporate in the terms of the minute for decree, after the words "in terms of the crave of the initial writ," the words "or such other sum (or sums) as the Court may think proper."

14. The minute for decree must be signed by a solicitor who has examined the affidavits and other documents and takes responsibility therefor, whether or not he is the person who drew the initial writ or affidavits.

15. In consent cases, the defender's written consent form will also have to be borrowed up, put to the pursuer in his or her affidavit, and docqueted and identified in the same way as other productions.

16. Affidavit procedure will not prevent the parties to the action agreeing the financial or other ancillary craves by joint minute. For so long as these ancillary craves are opposed, the affidavit procedure cannot be used for them, but it can be used for the merits of the action. If a joint minute is signed before an affidavit or supplementary affidavit is emitted by the pursuer, that affidavit must refer to the arrangements in the joint minute. Decree of divorce will not be granted before any issues relating to financial provisions consequent upon the divorce which require to be decided by the court, have been so decided.

17. Where the pursuer has craved a capital allowance, a periodical allowance, aliment for the child or children, or expenses, and in the minute for decree does not seek decree for one or any of these, it is essential that the reasons for this are fully narrated in the affidavit. Where these reasons are capable of corroboration by witnesses, they should be dealt with in the witnesses' affidavits.

[18. Solicitors are reminded that the normal rules of evidence about corroboration still apply except where:

(a) the action is brought in reliance on the facts set out in section 1(2)(*d*) (2 years non-cohabitation and the defender's consent to decree) or in section 1(2)(*e*) (5 years non-cohabitation) of the Divorce (Scotland) Act 1976;

(b) no other proceedings are pending in any court which could have the effect of bringing the marriage to an end;

(c) there are no children of the marriage under the age of 16 years;

(d) neither party applies for an order for financial provision on divorce; and

(e)   neither party suffers from mental disorder within
         the meaning of Section 6 of the Mental Health
         (Scotland) Act 1960.][4]

---

[4] Words in square brackets omitted from Sheriffdom of Lothian and Borders Act
of Court (Consolidation, etc.) 1990 No. 1 wherein there is substituted the
following: "While it is no longer necessary to corroborate any fact, proof of
which is required to establish a ground of divorce or any other matter, solicitors
are nonetheless reminded that any affidavit or affidavits must satisfy the
requirements of section 8 of the Civil Evidence (Scotland) Act 1988."

ORDINARY CAUSE FORMS RELATIVE TO DIVORCE ACTIONS

Form F1   **Rule 33.7(1)(a)**
FORM OF INTIMATION TO CHILDREN AND NEXT-OF-KIN IN AN ACTION
OF DIVORCE OR SEPARATION WHERE THE DEFENDER'S ADDRESS IS
NOT KNOWN

To (*insert name and address as in warrant*)   Court ref. no.

You are given NOTICE that an action of divorce [*or* separation] has been raised against (*insert name*) your (*insert relationship, e.g. father, mother, brother or other relative as the case may be*). If you know of his [*or* her] present address, you are requested to inform the sheriff clerk (*insert address of sheriff clerk*) in writing immediately. If you wish to appear as a party you must lodge a minute with the sheriff clerk for leave to do so. Your minute must be lodged within 21 days of (*insert date on which intimation was given. N.B. Rule 5.3 (2) relating to postal service or intimation*).

Date (*insert date*)   (*Signed*) A. B.
                         [Solicitor for the pursuer (*add designation and business address*)]

NOTE
If you decide to lodge a minute it may be in your best interest to consult a solicitor. The minute should be lodged with the sheriff clerk with the appropriate fee of (*insert amount*) and a copy of this intimation.

IF YOU ARE UNCERTAIN WHAT ACTION TO TAKE you should consult a solicitor. You may be entitled to legal aid depending on your financial circumstances, and you can get information about legal aid from a solicitor. You may also obtain advice from any Citizens Advice Bureau or other advice agency.

Form F2 **Rule 33.7(1)(b)**
FORM OF INTIMATION TO ALLEGED ADULTERER IN ACTION OF
DIVORCE OR SEPARATION

To (*insert name and address as in warrant*)   Court ref. no.

You are given NOTICE that in this action, you are alleged to have committed adultery. A copy of the initial writ is attached. If you wish to dispute the truth of the allegation made against you, you must lodge a minute with the sheriff clerk (*insert address of sheriff clerk*) for leave to appear as a party. Your minute must be lodged within 21 days of (*insert date on which intimation given. N.B. Rule 5.3(2) relating to postal service or intimation*).

Date (*insert date*)   (*Signed*) A.B.
                              [Solicitor for the pursuer]

NOTE
If you decide to lodge a minute it may be in your best interest to consult a solicitor. The minute should be lodged with the sheriff clerk together with the appropriate fee of (*insert amount*) and a copy of this intimation.

IF YOU ARE UNCERTAIN WHAT ACTION TO TAKE you should consult a solicitor. You may be entitled to legal aid depending on your financial circumstances, and you can get information about legal aid from a solicitor. You may also obtain advice from any Citizens Advice Bureau or other advice agency.

Form F3   **Rule 33.7(1)(c)**
FORM OF INTIMATION TO CHILDREN, NEXT OF KIN AND *CURATOR BONIS* IN AN ACTION OF DIVORCE OR SEPARATION WHERE THE DEFENDER SUFFERS FROM A MENTAL DISORDER

To (*insert name and address as in warrant*)   Court ref. no.

You are given NOTICE that an action of divorce [*or* separation] has been raised against (*insert name, and designation*) your (*insert relationship, e.g. father, mother, brother or other relative, or ward, as the case may be*). A copy of the initial writ is enclosed. If you wish to appear as a party, you must lodge a minute with the sheriff clerk (*insert address of sheriff clerk*), for leave to do so. Your minute must be lodged within 21 days of (*insert date on which intimation was given. N.B. Rule 5.3(2) relating to postal service or intimation*).

Date (*insert date*)   (*Signed*) A.B.
                                [Solicitor for the pursuer (*insert designation and business address*)]

NOTE
If you decide to lodge a minute it may be in your best interest to consult a solicitor. The minute should be lodged with the sheriff clerk together with the appropriate fee of (*insert amount*) and a copy of this intimation.

IF YOU ARE UNCERTAIN WHAT ACTION TO TAKE you should consult a solicitor. You may be entitled to legal aid depending on your financial circumstances, and you can get information about legal aid from a solicitor. You may also obtain advice from any Citizens Advice Bureau or other advice agency.

Form F4   **Rule 33.7(1)(d)**
FORM OF INTIMATION TO ADDITIONAL SPOUSE OF EITHER PARTY IN
PROCEEDINGS RELATING TO A POLYGAMOUS MARRIAGE

To (*name and address as in warrant*)   Court ref. no.

You are given NOTICE that this action for divorce [*or* separation], involves (*insert name and designation*) your spouse. A copy of the initial writ is attached. If you wish to appear as a party, you must lodge a minute with the sheriff clerk (*insert address of sheriff clerk*) for leave to do so. Your minute must be lodged within 21 days of (*insert date on which intimation was given. N.B. Rule 5.3(2) relating to postal service or intimation*).

Date (*insert date*)   (*Signed*) A.B.
                              [Solicitor for the pursuer]

NOTE
If you decide to lodge a minute it may be in your best interest to consult a solicitor. The minute should be lodged with the sheriff clerk with the appropriate fee of (*insert amount*) and a copy of this intimation.

IF YOU ARE UNCERTAIN WHAT ACTION TO TAKE you should consult a solicitor. You may be entitled to legal aid depending on your financial circumstances, and you can get information about legal aid from a solicitor. You may also obtain advice from any Citizens Advice Bureau or other advice agency.

Form F5   **Rule 33.7(1)(e)(i) and (ii)**
FORM OF INTIMATION TO A LOCAL AUTHORITY OR THIRD PARTY WHO
MAY BE LIABLE TO MAINTAIN A CHILD

To (*name and address as in warrant*)   Court ref. no.

You are given NOTICE that in this action, the court may make an order in respect of
the custody of (*insert name and address*), a child in your care [*or* liable to be
maintained by you]. A copy of the initial writ is attached. If you wish to appear as a
party, you must lodge a minute with the sheriff clerk (*insert address of sheriff clerk*)
for leave to do so. Your minute must be lodged within 21 days of (*insert date on
which intimation was given. N.B. Rule 5.3(2) relating to postal service or intimation*).

Date (*insert date*)   (*Signed*) A.B.
    [Solicitor for the pursuer]

NOTE
The minute should be lodged with the sheriff clerk with the appropriate fee of
(*insert amount*) and a copy of this intimation.

IF YOU ARE UNCERTAIN WHAT ACTION TO TAKE you should consult a solicitor. You
may be entitled to legal aid depending on your financial circumstances, and you
can get information about legal aid from a solicitor. You may also obtain advice
from any Citizens Advice Bureau or other advice agency.

Form F6   **Rule 33.7(1)(e)(iii)**
FORM OF INTIMATION TO PERSON HAVING *DE FACTO* CUSTODY OF A
CHILD

To (*name and address as in warrant*)   Court ref. no.

You are given NOTICE that in this action, the court may make an order in respect of the custody of (*insert name and address*) a child at present in your custody. A copy of the initial writ is attached. If you wish to appear as a party, you must lodge a minute with the sheriff clerk (*insert address of sheriff clerk*) for leave to do so. Your minute must be lodged within 21 days of (*insert date on which intimation was given. N.B. Rule 5.3(2) relating to postal service or intimation*).

Date (*insert date*)   (*Signed*) A.B.
                                  [Solicitor for the pursuer]

NOTE
If you decide to lodge a minute it may be in your best interest to consult a solicitor. The minute should be lodged with the sheriff clerk with the appropriate fee of (*insert amount*) and a copy of this intimation.

IF YOU ARE UNCERTAIN WHAT ACTION TO TAKE you should consult a solicitor. You may be entitled to legal aid depending on your financial circumstances, and you can get information about legal aid from a solicitor. You may also obtain advice from any Citizens Advice Bureau or other advice agency.

Form F7   **Rules 33.7(1)(f) and 33.19(1)(a)(i)**
FORM OF NOTICE TO PARENT OR GUARDIAN IN ACTION FOR CUSTODY
OF A CHILD

1. You are given NOTICE that in this action, the pursuer seeks custody of the child (*insert name of child*). A copy of the initial writ is served on you and is attached to this notice.

2. *The pursuer, being a relative [*or* step parent] of the child, has the consent of [*or* seeks the consent of] (*insert name of parent or guardian*) who is a parent [*or* guardian] of the child, and has had care and possession of the child for three months preceding the lodging of the initial writ on (*insert date*);
OR
*The pursuer has the consent of [*or* seeks the consent of] (*insert name of parent or guardian*) who is a parent [*or* guardian] of the child and has had care and possession of the child, for a period or periods before lodging the writ which amount to at least twelve months including the three months preceding the lodging of the initial writ on (*insert date*).
OR
*The pursuer has had care and possession of the child for a period before the lodging of this writ which amount to at least three years, including the three years preceding the lodging of the initial writ on (*insert date*).
OR
*The pursuer intends to establish the following as showing cause why the pursuer should be granted custody of the child (*state briefly the ground on which custody is sought or refer to the relevant article of condescendence in the writ*).
   *Delete as appropriate.

3.*If you wish to consent to the pursuer being granted custody of the child in the event of the court deciding that that was appropriate, you should complete Form F25.
OR
*(*Insert name of parent or guardian*) has consented to the pursuer being granted custody of the child in the event of the court deciding that that was appropriate.
   *Both alternative paragraphs should be struck out if the pursuer is a parent or guardian.

[*Insert if appropriate*   AND
The writ states that the child has been in the care and possession of the pursuer for a period or periods which amount to three years and accordingly, if that is correct, it is an offence to remove the child from the custody of the pursuer against the will of the pursuer except with the authority of the court or under the authority of any enactment or on the lawful arrest of the child.]

4. If you wish to oppose this action, and oppose the granting of custody of the child to the pursuer, you must lodge a notice of intention to defend (Form F26). See Form F26 attached for further details.

Date (*insert date*)   (*Signed*)
                               A.B., Pursuer
                               or X.Y. [Solicitor for the pursuer (*add designation and business address*)]

NOTE

IF YOU ARE UNCERTAIN WHAT ACTION TO TAKE you should consult a solicitor. You may be entitled to legal aid depending on your financial circumstances, and you can get information about legal aid from a solicitor. You may also obtain advice from any Citizens Advice Bureau or other advice agency.

Form F8   **Rules 33.7(1)(g), 33.7(4) and 33.12(2)**
FORM OF NOTICE TO LOCAL AUTHORITY UNDER SECTION 49(1) OF THE
CHILDREN ACT 1975

To (*insert name and address*)   Court ref. no.

1. You are given NOTICE that the pursuer has presented an initial writ to the sheriff
court at (*insert address*) for the custody of the child (*insert name of child*). A copy of
the initial writ is enclosed.

2. You are required under section 49(2) of the Children Act 1975 to submit to the
court a report on all the circumstances of the child and on the proposed
arrangements for the care and upbringing of the child.

Date (*insert date*)   (*Signed*) A.B.
                                  [Solicitor for the pursuer (*add designation and
                                  business address*)]

FORM OF INTIMATION IN AN ACTION WHICH AFFECTS A CHILD

To (*name and address as in warrant*)   Court ref. no.

You are given NOTICE that in this action the pursuer craves the court to (*insert details of the crave(s) that affect the child*) which affect you. A copy of the initial writ is attached. If you wish to appear as a party, you must lodge a minute with the sheriff clerk (*insert address of sheriff clerk*) for leave to do so. Your minute must be lodged within 21 days of (*insert date on which intimation was given. N.B. Rule 5.3(2) relating to postal service or intimation*).

Date (*insert date*)   (*Signed*) A.B.
                                        [Solicitor for the pursuer]

NOTE
If you decide to lodge a minute it may be in your best interest to consult a solicitor. The minute should be lodged with the sheriff clerk with the appropriate fee of (*insert amount*) and a copy of this intimation.

IF YOU ARE UNCERTAIN WHAT ACTION TO TAKE you should consult a solicitor. You may be entitled to legal aid depending on your financial circumstances, and you can get information about legal aid from a solicitor. You may also obtain advice from any Citizens Advice Bureau or other advice agency.

Form F10   **Rule 33.7(1)(i)**

FORM OF INTIMATION TO CREDITOR IN APPLICATION FOR ORDER FOR
THE TRANSFER OF PROPERTY UNDER SECTION 8 OF THE FAMILY LAW
(SCOTLAND) ACT 1985

To (*insert name and address as in warrant*)   Court ref. no.

You are given NOTICE that in this action an order is sought for the transfer of
property (*specify the order*), over which you hold a security. A copy of the initial
writ is attached. If you wish to appear as a party, you must lodge a minute with the
sheriff clerk (*insert address of sheriff clerk*) for leave to do so. Your minute must be
lodged within 21 days of (*insert date on which intimation was given. N.B. Rule 5.3(2)
relating to postal service or intimation*).

Date (*insert date*)   (*Signed*) A.B.
                                   [Solicitor for the pursuer]

NOTE
If you decide to lodge a minute it may be in your best interest to consult a solicitor.
The minute should be lodged with the sheriff clerk with the appropriate fee of
(*insert amount*) and a copy of this intimation.

IF YOU ARE UNCERTAIN WHAT ACTION TO TAKE you should consult a solicitor. You
may be entitled to legal aid depending on your financial circumstances, and you
can get information about legal aid from a solicitor. You may also obtain advice
from any Citizens Advice Bureau or other advice agency.

Form F11   **Rule 33.7(1)(j)**
FORM OF INTIMATION IN AN ACTION WHERE THE PURSUER MAKES AN
APPLICATION FOR AN ORDER UNDER SECTION 18 OF THE FAMILY LAW
(SCOTLAND) ACT 1985

To (*insert name and address as in warrant*)   Court ref. no.

You are given NOTICE that in this action, the pursuer craves the court to make an
order under section 18 of the Family Law (Scotland) Act 1985. A copy of the initial
writ is attached. If you wish to appear as a party, you must lodge a minute with the
sheriff clerk (*insert address of sheriff clerk*) for leave to do so. Your minute must be
lodged within 21 days of (*insert date on which intimation was given. N.B. Rule 5.3(2)
relating to postal service or intimation*).

Date (*insert date*)   (*Signed*) A.B.
                              [Solicitor for the pursuer]

NOTE
If you decide to lodge a minute it may be in your best interest to consult a solicitor.
The minute should be lodged with the sheriff clerk with the appropriate fee of
(*insert amount*) and a copy of this intimation.

IF YOU ARE UNCERTAIN WHAT ACTION TO TAKE you should consult a solicitor. You
may be entitled to legal aid depending on your financial circumstances, and you
can get information about legal aid from a solicitor. You may also obtain advice
from any Citizens Advice Bureau or other advice agency.

Form F12 **Rule 33.7(1)(k)**
FORM OF INTIMATION IN AN ACTION WHERE A NON-ENTITLED
PURSUER MAKES AN APPLICATION FOR AN ORDER UNDER THE
MATRIMONIAL HOMES (FAMILY PROTECTION) (SCOTLAND) ACT 1981

To (*insert name and address as in warrant*)   Court ref. no.

You are given NOTICE that in this action, the pursuer craves the court to make an order under section of (*insert the section under which the order(s) sought*) of the Matrimonial Homes (Family Protection) (Scotland)Act 1981. A copy of the initial writ is attached. If you wish to appear as a party, you must lodge a minute with the sheriff clerk (*insert address of sheriff clerk*) for leave to do so. Your minute must be lodged within 21 days of (*insert date on which intimation was given. N.B. Rule 5.3(2) relating to postal service or intimation*).

Date (*insert date*)   (*Signed*) A.B.
                              [Solicitor for the pursuer]

NOTE
If you decide to lodge a minute it may be in your best interest to consult a solicitor. The minute should be lodged with the sheriff clerk with the appropriate fee of (*insert amount*) and a copy of this intimation.

IF YOU ARE UNCERTAIN WHAT ACTION TO TAKE you should consult a solicitor. You may be entitled to legal aid depending on your financial circumstances, and you can get information about legal aid from a solicitor. You may also obtain advice from any Citizens Advice Bureau or other advice agency.

Form F13   **Rule 33.8(3)**
FORM OF INTIMATION TO PERSON WITH WHOM AN IMPROPER
ASSOCIATION IS ALLEGED TO HAVE OCCURRED

To (*insert name and address as in warrant*)   Court ref. no.

You are given NOTICE that in this action, the defender is alleged to have had an improper association with you. A copy of the initial writ is attached. If you wish to dispute the truth of the allegation made against you, you must lodge a minute with the sheriff clerk (*insert address of sheriff clerk*) for leave to appear as a party. Your minute must be lodged within 21 days of (*insert date on which intimation was given. N.B. Rule 5.3(2) relating to postal service or intimation*).

Date (*insert date*)   (*Signed*) A.B.
                                      [Solicitor for the pursuer]

NOTE
If you decide to lodge a minute it may be in your best interest to consult a solicitor. The minute should be lodged with the sheriff clerk with the appropriate fee of (*insert amount*) and a copy of this intimation.

IF YOU ARE UNCERTAIN WHAT ACTION TO TAKE you should consult a solicitor. You may be entitled to legal aid depending on your financial circumstances, and you can get information about legal aid from a solicitor. You may also obtain advice from any Citizens Advice Bureau or other advice agency.

Form F14 **Rule 33.10**
FORM OF WARRANT OF CITATION IN FAMILY ACTION

(*Insert place and date*)
Grants warrant to cite the defender (*insert name and address of defender*) by serving upon him [*or* her] a copy of the writ and warrant upon a period of notice of (*insert period of notice*) days, and ordains the defender to lodge a notice of intention to defend with the sheriff clerk at (*insert address of sheriff court*) if he [*or* she] wishes to:

    (a)   challenge the jurisdiction of the court;
    (b)   oppose any claim made or order sought;
    (c)   make any claim or seek any order.

[Meantime grants interim interdict, *or* warrant to arrest on the dependence].

Form F15   **Rules 33.11(1) and 33.13(1)(a)**
FORM OF CITATION IN FAMILY ACTION

CITATION

SHERIFFDOM OF (*insert name of sheriffdom*)
AT (*insert place of sheriff court*)

[A.B.], (*insert designation and address*) Pursuer, against [C.D.], (*insert designation and address*), Defender.
    Court ref. no.

(*Insert place and date*) You [C.D.] are hereby served with this copy writ and warrant, with Form F26 (notice of intention to defend) [and (*insert details of any other form of notice served, e.g. any of the forms served in accordance with rule 33.14*].

FORM F26 is served on you for use should you wish to intimate an intention to defend the action.

IF YOU WISH TO—
    (a)   challenge the jurisdiction of the court;
    (b)   oppose any claim made or order sought;
    (c)   make any claim or seek any order; or
    (d)   seek any order;
you should consult a solicitor with a view to lodging a notice of intention to defend (Form F26). The notice of intention to defend, together with the court fee of £(*insert amount*) must be lodged with the sheriff clerk at the above address within 21 days (*or insert appropriate period of notice*) of (*insert the date on which service was executed. N.B. Rule 5.3(2) relating to postal service or intimation*).

IF YOU ARE UNCERTAIN WHAT ACTION TO TAKE you should consult a solicitor. You may be entitled to legal aid depending on your financial circumstances, and you can get information about legal aid from a solicitor. You may also obtain advice from any Citizens Advice Bureau or other advice agency.

PLEASE NOTE THAT IF YOU DO NOTHING IN ANSWER TO THIS DOCUMENT the court may regard you as admitting the claim made against you and the pursuer may obtain decree against you in your absence.

                        (*Signed*)
                        [P.Q.]., Sheriff officer
                        or
                        [X.Y.] (*add designation and business address*)
                        Solicitor for the pursuer

Form F16   **Rule 33.11(2)**

FORM OF CERTIFICATE OF CITATION IN FAMILY ACTION

CERTIFICATE OF CITATION

(*Insert place and date*) I,   hereby certify that upon the   day of   I duly cited [C.D.], Defender, to answer to the foregoing writ. This I did by (*state method of service; if by officer and not by post, add:* in presence of [L.M.], (*insert designation*)), witness hereto with me subscribing; and (*insert details of any forms of intimation or notice sent including details of the person to whom intimation sent and the method of service*).

                           (*Signed*)
                           [P.Q.], Sheriff officer
                           [L.M.], witness
                           or
                           [X.Y.], (*add designation and business address*)
                           Solicitor for the pursuer

Form F17   **Rule 33.13(1)(c)**
FORM OF REQUEST TO MEDICAL OFFICER OF HOSPITAL OR SIMILAR
INSTITUTION

To (*insert name and address of medical officer*)
In terms of rule 33.13(1)(*c*) of the Ordinary Cause Rules of the Sheriff Court a copy
of the initial writ at the instance of (*insert name and address of pursuer*), Pursuer,
against (*insert name and address of defender*), Defender, is enclosed and you are
requested to
(a) deliver it personally to the (*insert name of defender*), and
(b) explain the contents to him or her,
unless you are satisfied that such delivery of explanation would be dangerous to
his or her health or mental condition. You are further requested to complete and
return to me in the enclosed stamped addressed envelope the certificate appended
hereto, making necessary deletions.

Date (*insert date*)   (*Signed*) A.B.
                                      [Solicitor for the pursuer (*add designation and
                                      business address*)]

Form F18 **Rules 33.13(1)(d) and 33.13(2)**
FORM OF CERTIFICATE BY MEDICAL OFFICER OF HOSPITAL OR SIMILAR
INSTITUTION

Court ref. no.

I (*insert name and designation*) certify that I have received a copy initial writ in an
action of (*type of family action to be inserted by the party requesting service*) at the
instance of (*insert name and designation*), Pursuer, against (*insert name and
designation*), Defender, and that
*I have on the   day of   personally delivered a copy thereof to the said
defender who is under my care at (*insert address*) and I have explained the contents
or purport thereof to him or her, *or*
*I have not delivered a copy thereof to the said defender who is under my care at
(*insert address*) and I have not explained the contents or purport thereof to him or
her because (*state reasons*).

Date (*insert date*)   (*Signed*) A.B.
                              [Medical officer (*add designation and address*)]

*Delete as appropriate.

Form F19   **Rule 33.14(1)(a)(i)**

FORM OF NOTICE TO DEFENDER WHERE IT IS STATED THAT DEFENDER
CONSENTS TO THE GRANTING OF DECREE OF DIVORCE

You are given NOTICE that the copy initial writ served on you with this notice states that you consent to the grant of decree of divorce.

1. If you do so consent the consequences for you are that—

    (a)   provided the pursuer establishes the fact that he [*or* she] has not cohabited with you at any time during a continuous period of two years after the date of your marriage and immediately preceding the bringing of this action and that you consent, a decree of divorce will be granted;

    (b)   on the grant of a decree of divorce you may lose your rights of succession to the pursuer's estate; and

    (c)   decree of divorce will end the marriage thereby affecting any right to such pension as may depend on the marriage continuing, or, on your being left a widow the state widow's pension will not be payable to you when the pursuer dies.

Apart from these, there may be other consequences for you depending upon your particular circumstances.

2. You are entitled, whether or not you consent to the grant of decree to apply to the sheriff in this action—

    (a)   to make financial or other provision for you under the Family Law (Scotland) Act 1985;

    (b)   for an order under the Law Reform (Parent and Child) (Scotland) Act 1986 relating to parental rights (including custody and access) to any child of the marriage, or any child accepted as such, who is under 16 years of age; or

    (c)   for any other competent order.

3. IF YOU WISH TO APPLY FOR ANY OF THE ABOVE ORDERS you should consult a solicitor with a view to lodging a notice of intention to defend (Form F26).

4. If, after consideration, you wish to consent to decree, you should complete and sign the attached form of notice of consent (Form F20) and send it to the sheriff clerk at the sheriff court referred to in the initial writ within 21 days of (*insert the date on which service was executed. N.B. Rule 5.3(2) relating to postal service*).

5. If at a later stage you wish to withdraw your consent you must inform the sheriff clerk immediately in writing that you withdraw your consent to decree being granted against you in this action.

Date (*insert date*)   (*Signed*) A.B.

                                         [Solicitor for the pursuer (*add designation and business address*)]

Form F20   **Rule 33.14(1)(a)(i) and 33.18(1)**

Court ref. no.

FORM OF NOTICE OF CONSENT IN ACTIONS OF DIVORCE UNDER
SECTION 1(2)(D) OF THE DIVORCE (SCOTLAND) ACT 1976

[A.B.], (*insert designation and address*), Pursuer, against [C.D.], (*insert designation and address*), Defender

I (*full name and address of the defender to be inserted by pursuer or pursuer's solicitor before sending notice*) have received a copy of the initial writ in the action against me at the instance of (*full name and address of pursuer to be inserted by pursuer or pursuer's solicitor before sending notice*). I understand that it states that I consent to the grant of decree of divorce in this action. I have considered the consequences for me mentioned in the notice (Form F19) sent to me with this notice. I consent to the grant of decree of divorce in this action.

Date (*insert date*)   (*Signed*) A.B.
                              [Defender]

FORM OF NOTICE TO DEFENDER WHERE IT IS STATED THAT DEFENDER
CONSENTS TO THE GRANTING OF DECREE OF SEPARATION

You are given NOTICE that the copy initial writ served on you with this notice states that you consent to the grant of decree of separation.
1. If you do so consent the consequences for you are that—
  (a)   provided the pursuer establishes the fact that he [*or* she] has not cohabited with you at any time during a continuous period of two years after the date of your marriage and immediately preceding the bringing of this action and that you consent, a decree of separation will be granted;
  (b)   on the grant of decree of separation you will be obliged to live apart from the pursuer but the marriage will continue to subsist; you will continue to have a legal obligation to support your wife [*or* husband] and children;
Apart from these, there may be other consequences for you depending upon your particular circumstances.

2. If you do consent to the grant of decree you may apply to the sheriff in this action—
  (a)   to make financial or other provision for you under the Family Law (Scotland) Act 1985;
  (b)   for an order under the Law Reform (Parent and Child) (Scotland) Act 1986 relating to parental rights (including custody and access) to any child of the marriage, or any child accepted as such, who is under 16 years of age; or
  (c)   for any other competent order.

3. IF YOU WISH TO APPLY FOR ANY OF THE ABOVE ORDERS you should consult a solicitor with a view to lodging a notice of intention to defend (Form F26).

4. If after consideration, you wish to consent to decree, you should complete and sign the attached Form of notice of consent (Form F22) and send it to the sheriff clerk at the sheriff court referred to in the initial writ and other papers within 21 days of (*insert the date on which service was executed. N.B. Rule 5.3(2) relating to postal service or intimation*).

5. If at a later stage you wish to withdraw your consent you must inform the sheriff clerk immediately in writing that you withdraw your consent to decree being granted against you in this action.

Date (*insert date*)   (*Signed*) A.B.
                              [Solicitor for the pursuer (*add designation and business address*)]

Form F22   **Rules 33.14(1)(a)(ii) and 33.18(1)**

Court ref. no.

FORM OF NOTICE OF CONSENT IN ACTIONS OF SEPARATION UNDER SECTION 1(2)(D) OF THE DIVORCE (SCOTLAND) ACT 1976

[A.B.], *(insert designation and address)*, Pursuer against [C.D.], *(insert designation and address)*, Defender

I *(full name and address of the defender to be inserted by pursuer or pursuer's solicitor before sending notice)* confirm that I have received a copy of the initial writ in the action against me at the instance of *(full name and address of pursuer to be inserted by pursuer or pursuer's solicitor before sending notice)*. I understand that it states that I consent to the grant of decree of separation in this action. I have considered the consequences for me mentioned in the notice (Form F21) sent together with this notice. I consent to the grant of decree of separation in this action.

Date *(insert date)*   *(Signed)* A.B.
                                          [Defender]

Form F23   **Rule 33.14(1)(b)(i)**
FORM OF NOTICE TO DEFENDER IN AN ACTION OF DIVORCE WHERE IT
IS STATED THERE HAS BEEN FIVE YEARS' NON-COHABITATION

You are given NOTICE that—

1. The copy initial writ served on you with this notice states that there has been no cohabitation between you and the pursuer at any time during a continuous period of five years after the date of the marriage and immediately preceding the commencement of this action. If the pursuer establishes this as a fact and the sheriff is satisfied that the marriage has broken down irretrievably, a decree will be granted, unless the sheriff is of the opinion that to grant decree would result in grave financial hardship to you.

2. Decree of divorce will end the marriage thereby affecting any right to such pension as may depend on the marriage continuing, or, on your being left a widow the state widow's pension will not be payable to you when the pursuer dies. You may also lose your rights of succession to the pursuer's estate.

3. You are entitled, whether or not you dispute that there has been no such cohabitation during that five-year period, to apply to the sheriff in this action—
  (a)   to make financial or other provision for you under the Family Law (Scotland) Act 1985;
  (b)   for an order under the Law Reform (Parent and Child) (Scotland) Act 1986 relating to parental rights (including custody and access) to any child of the marriage, or any child accepted as such, who is under 16 years of age; or
  (c)   for any other competent order.

4. IF YOU WISH TO APPLY FOR ANY OF THE ABOVE ORDERS you should consult a solicitor with a view to lodging a notice of intention to defend (Form F26).

Date (*insert date*)   (*Signed*) A.B.
    [Solicitor for the pursuer (*add designation and business address*)]

Form F24   **Rule 33.14(1)(b)(ii)**
FORM OF NOTICE TO DEFENDER IN AN ACTION OF SEPARATION
WHERE IT IS STATED THERE HAS BEEN FIVE YEARS' NON-
COHABITATION

You are given NOTICE that—

1. The copy initial writ served on you together with this notice states that there has
ben no cohabitation between you and the pursuer at any time during a continuous
period of five years after the date of the marriage and immediately preceding the
commencement of this action and that if the pursuer establishes this as a fact, and
the sheriff is satisfied that there are grounds justifying decree of separation, a
decree will be granted, unless the sheriff is of the opinion that to grant decree
would result in grave financial hardship to you.

2. On the granting of decree of separation you will be obliged to live apart from the
pursuer but the marriage will continue to subsist. You will continue to have a legal
obligation to support your wife [*or* husband] and children.

3. You are entitled, whether or not you dispute that there has been no such
cohabitation during that five year period, to apply to the sheriff in this action—
   (a)   to make provision under the Family Law (Scotland) Act 1985;
   (b)   for an order under the Law Reform (Parent and Child) (Scotland) Act
         1986 relating to parental rights (including custody and access) to any
         child of the marriage, or any child accepted as such, who is under 16
         years of age; or
   (d)   for any other competent order.

   4. IF YOU WISH TO APPLY FOR ANY OF THE ABOVE ORDERS you should consult
   a solicitor with a view to lodging a notice of intention to defend (Form
   F26).

Date (*insert date*)   (*Signed*) A.B.
                                     [Solicitor for the pursuer (*add designation and
                                     business address*)]

Form F25 **Rules 33.19(1)(a)(ii) and 33.19(2)(i)**

FORM OF CONSENT OF PARENT OR GUARDIAN IN PROCEEDINGS FOR CUSTODY OF CHILDREN UNDER SECTION 47 OF THE CHILDREN ACT 1975

Court ref. no.

[A.B.], (*insert designation and address*), Pursuer, against [C.D.], (*insert designation and address*), Defender

I, (*insert name and address*) confirm that I am the mother [*or* father *or* guardian] of the child (*insert full name of the child as given on birth certificate, and the child's present address*). I understand that if I consent to the granting of custody to the pursuer, the care, possession and control of the child may be granted to the pursuer by the court. I hereby consent to the making of a custody order in relation to the child (*insert name of child*) in favour of (*insert name and address of pursuer*).

Dated at (*insert place*) on the   day of   19 .

Signature of person consenting ....

Signature of Witness .... Signature of Witness ....

*Full Name .... *Full Name ....

*Designation .... *Designation ....

*Address .... *Address ....

....

   *Please complete in block capitals.

Form F26   **Rules 33.11(1) and 33.34(2)**

FORM OF NOTICE OF INTENTION TO DEFEND IN A FAMILY ACTION

NOTICE OF INTENTION TO DEFEND

*PART A

Court ref. no.

(*Insert name and business address of solicitor for the pursuer*)	In an action raised at Sheriff Court
	....
Solicitor for the pursuer	....
	....
Pursuer	
	....
	....
	....
	Defender

*(THIS SECTION TO BE COMPLETED
BY THE PURSUER BEFORE SERVICE)

DATE OF SERVICE: DATE OF EXPIRY OF PERIOD OF NOTICE:
*PART B

*(THIS SECTION TO BE COMPLETED BY THE DEFENDER OR DEFENDER'S SOLICITOR, AND
BOTH PARTS OF THE FORM RETURNED TO THE SHERIFF CLERK AT THE ABOVE SHERIFF
COURT ON OR BEFORE THE DATE OF EXPIRY OF THE PERIOD OF NOTICE REFERRED TO IN
PART A ABOVE.)

(*Insert place and date*)

[C.D.] (*insert designation and address*), Defender, intends to
- (a)   challenge the jurisdiction of the court;
- (b)   oppose a crave in the initial writ;
- (c)   make a claim;
- (d)   seek an order;

in the action against him or her raised by [A.B.], (*insert designation and address*),
Pursuer, against him [*or* her].

> (*Signed*)
> [C.D.], Defender
> *or*[X.Y.], (*add designation and business address*)
> Solicitor for the defender

Form F27   **Rule 33.29(1)(b)**
FORM OF MINUTE FOR DECREE IN FAMILY ACTION TO WHICH RULE
33.28 APPLIES

(*Insert name of solicitor for the pursuer*) having considered the evidence contained in the affidavits and the other documents all as specified in the schedule hereto, and being satisfied that upon the evidence a motion for decree (in terms of the crave of the initial writ) [*or in such restricted terms as may be appropriate*] may properly be made, moves the court accordingly.

In respect whereof

(*Signed*) A.B.
[Solicitor for the pursuer (*add designation and business address*)]

SCHEDULE
(*Number and specify documents considered*)

Form F28   **Rules 33.40(c) and 33.64(1)(c)**
FORM OF NOTICE OF INTIMATION TO LOCAL AUTHORITY OR THIRD
PARTY TO WHOM CARE OF A CHILD IS TO BE GIVEN

To (*name and address as in warrant*)   Court ref. no.

You are given NOTICE that in this action, the sheriff proposes to commit to your care the child (*insert name and address*). A copy of the initial writ is attached. If you wish to appear as a party, you must lodge a minute with the sheriff clerk (*insert address of sheriff clerk*) for leave to do so. Your minute must be lodged within 21 days of (*insert date on which intimation was given. N.B. Rule 5.3(2) relating to postal service or intimation*).

Date (*insert date*)   (*Signed*) A.B.
                                  [Solicitor for the pursuer]

NOTE
If you decide to lodge a minute it may be in your best interest to consult a solicitor. The minute should be lodged with the sheriff clerk with the appropriate fee of (*insert amount*) and a copy of this intimation.

IF YOU ARE UNCERTAIN WHAT ACTION TO TAKE you should consult a solicitor. You may be entitled to legal aid depending on your financial circumstances, and you can get information about legal aid from a solicitor. You may also obtain advice from any Citizens Advice Bureau or other advice agency.

Form F29   **Rules 33.41 and 33.64(2)**
FORM OF NOTICE OF INTIMATION TO LOCAL AUTHORITY OF
SUPERVISION ORDER

[A.B.], *(insert designation and address)*, Pursuer, against [C.D.], *(insert designation and address)*, Defender

To *(insert name and address of local authority)*   Court ref. no.

You are given NOTICE that on *(insert date)* in the Sheriff Court at *(insert place)* the sheriff made a supervision order under section 12 of the Matrimonial Proceedings (Children) Act 1958 [*or* section 11(1)(b) of the Guardianship Act 1973] placing the child *(insert name and address of child)* under your supervision. A certified copy of the sheriff's interlocutor is attached.

Date *(insert date)*   *(Signed)*
                              [Sheriff clerk (depute)]

168 *Ordinary Cause Forms Relative to Divorce Actions*

Form F30   **Rules 33.72(1) and 33.72(2)**
FORM OF CERTIFICATE OF DELIVERY OF DOCUMENTS TO CHIEF
CONSTABLE

(*Insert place and date*) I,   hereby certify that upon the   day of   I duly
delivered to (*insert name and address*) chief constable of (*insert name of constabulary*)
(*insert details of the documents delivered*). This I did by (*state method of service*).

(*Signed*) A.B.
[Solicitor for the pursuer (*add designation and business address*)]

INFORMATION REQUIRED FOR ACTUARIAL VALUATIONS RELATIVE TO SECTION 10(5) OF THE FAMILY LAW (SCOTLAND) ACT 1985[1]

A. Defined Benefit Pension Schemes

(i) Basic Information Required for Actuarial Valuation

Name of scheme member ....

(a) Dates of birth of both parties

Member of scheme ....

Spouse ....

(b) Date of marriage ....

(c) Relevant Date for the purposes of the Act. This is defined to mean the earlier of:
"The date on which the parties cease to cohabit or the date of service of the summons"

....

---

[1] This Appendix has been compiled by Messrs R. Watson & Sons, Consulting Actuaries, 11 Abercromby Place, Edinburgh.

(d) A full description of scheme benefits. A member's explanatory booklet will usually give these details

Name of Scheme ....

Booklet enclosed   YES/NO

(e) Details of the Trustees'/Employer's policy regarding pension increases. (The explanatory booklet will almost certainly give details of any guaranteed increases, but there may be a practice of giving discretionary increases. If so, a statement of practice, or details of the increases granted in the past few years should be given.)

....

....

(f) Date of commencement of pensionable service

....

(g) Member's pensionable salary as at the Relevant Date

....

(h) Deferred pension that would have been available if the member had left the scheme on the Relevant Date

....

(i) Transfer value that would have been available if the member had left the scheme on the Relevant Date

....

(j) If the Scheme is contracted-out of the State Earnings Related Pension Scheme (SERPS), the accrued Guaranteed Minimum Pension (GMP) as at the Relevant Date with a note of the part attributable to service after 5 April 1988. If this is not available, contracted-out rate National Insurance contributions or Relevant Earnings paid for each fiscal year to the Relevant Date

....

(k) Ordinary   member's   contributions   to   the   scheme
     accumulated with interest to the Relevant Date

....

(l)   Details of any additional voluntary contributions paid to the
     scheme and any benefits deriving therefrom

....

(m) Details of any transfer payments made to the scheme and the
     benefits deriving therefrom

....

(n) Is   the   member   still   an   employed   member   of   the
     scheme?   YES/NO

     If not, what benefits were granted on leaving or retirement

....

(ii) Notes on Basic Information Required for Actuarial Valuation

For some items it may be easier to attach a copy of a document
giving the required information than to enter the information on
the form. If you do this, please indicate accordingly on the form.

The lettering of the notes below corresponds to that of the items
on the form.

(d) If the scheme is the Principal Civil Service Pension Scheme, a
     Local Authority Superannuation Scheme, the Police or
     Firemen's Pension Scheme or the National Health Service
     (Scotland) Superannuation Scheme, we do not require
     details of the scheme's benefits.

     In some other cases also we may already have details of the
     scheme's benefits. If you have difficulty in obtaining an
     explanatory booklet please contact us to see if we already
     have details.

(e)   For the schemes listed in the first paragraph of note (d) we do not require details of the pension increase policy.

(g)   If the salary at the Relevant Date is not available, please quote a figure at a date as close to the Relevant Date as possible.

The salary must correspond with the definition of pensionable salary used by the scheme. For example, if the scheme uses only basic pay please ensure that you do not quote full taxable earnings.

If possible please supply the rate of salary at the Relevant Date. If you obtain this information from the member's scheme, you may be supplied with an average salary over the preceding year or three years, in accordance with the rules of the scheme. This is acceptable, but please ensure it is clear that this is how the salary has been calculated.

Some schemes make a deduction from salary for pension purposes to allow for the Basic State Pension. Please supply the salary before such deduction; if this is not possible please add a note to that effect.

(h)   This item is not essential but forms a valuable cross-check on the other information and should therefore be provided if possible.

(i)   This item is not essential for public sector schemes.

(j)   This item should be provided if possible. However, in practice we have found that some schemes are unable or unwilling to provide this information. If this is the case we can estimate this item.

(k)   In some schemes the amount of the member's contributions has no direct effect on the amount of the benefits, and even in others it has only a small effect. Therefore this item is not essential.

(l)   If no details are provided we shall assume that the member has not paid any voluntary contributions.

(m) If no details are provided we shall assume that there has been no transfer payment made.

B. Life Assurance and Personal Pension Policies

(i) Basic Information Required for Actuarial Valuation

Name of policy holder ....

(a) Dates of birth of both parties

Policy holder ....

Spouse...

(b) Date of Marriage ....

(c) Relevant Date for the purposes of the Act. This is defined to mean the earlier of:
"The date on which the parties cease to cohabit or the date of service of the summons"

....

(d) Insurance Company and Policy Number

....

(e) A copy of the policy document

Enclosed   YES/NO

(f) If the policy is a with-profits policy, a copy of the latest bonus declaration statement issued before the Relevant Date, the one first issued after the Relevant Date and the most recent one issued

Enclosed for years ....

(g) If the policy is a unit-linked policy, a copy of any statement of

unit values issued to the policy holder at the Relevant Date
or as close to it as possible and the most recent one issued

Enclosed as at ....

(h)   The surrender value (or transfer value) at the Relevant Date;
failing this, the surrender value (or transfer value) at a date
as close to the Relevant Date as possible

....

(ii) Life Assurance and Personal Pension Policies

Notes on Basic Information Required for Actuarial Valuation

The lettering of the notes below corresponds to that of the items
on the form.

(d)   If you require more than one policy valued, please complete
a separate form for each one, although naturally items (a) to
(c) need only be completed once.

(b)   If you cannot supply a copy of the policy document, please
supply the following information:

1.   Date the first premium was paid.

2.   Amount and frequency of premiums, stating whether
gross or net of Life Assurance Premium Relief.

3.   Original sum assured or benefit payable on retirement.

4.   Maturity or retirement date (if applicable).

5.   Any minimum sum payable on death before maturity or
retirement.

6.   Any other details which would affect the amount of
benefit paid in any circumstances.

(f)   If bonus declarations cannot be supplied for with-profit policies, we will attempt to ascertain the relevant information from the insurance company concerned. However, this is likely to be a time-consuming and hence costly exercise. In such circumstances it may be helpful to have a letter of authority from the policy holder to the insurance company.

(h) If the policy is a personal pension or retirement annuity policy, it will almost certainly not be possible to surrender it and the insurance company may reply to a request for a surrender value accordingly. For such policies you should instead request a transfer value. Some insurance companies may only quote a surrender value or transfer value as at the current date; however, in the first instance, you should request the value as at the Relevant Date.

TABLE OF MATRIMONIAL PROPERTY AND RESOURCES[1]

PURSUER	£	DEFENDER	£
At relevant date:		*At relevant date:*	
(i) One-half interest in matrimonial home	96,937	(i) one-half interest in matrimonial home	96,937
(ii) one-half interest in Scottish Widows Insurance Policy	3,684	(ii) one-half interest in Scottish Widows Insurance Policy	3,684
(iii) 38.03% interest in C.C. Hornig & Son Ltd. Executive Pension Fund	43,318	(iii) 61.97% interest in C.C. Hornig & Son Ltd. Executive Pension Fund	70,588
		(iv) interest in Legal & General Pension Plan Policy	4,000
		(v) interest in Liverpool and Victoria Insurance Policy	2,200
		(vi) cash in Bank of Scotland	3,567.32
		(vii) shares in C.C. Hornig & Son Ltd	69,000
SUBTOTAL	**143,939**	**SUBTOTAL**	**249,976.32**
Less		*Less*	
(a) one-half liability to Bank of Scotland	1,763.71	(a) one-half liability to Bank of Scotland	1,763.71
TOTAL	**142,175.29**	**TOTAL**	**248,212.61**

[1] This is the table (revised) presented to the Court on behalf of the defender in *Crockett* v. *Crockett*, 1992 S.C.L.R. 591.

At present date:	£	At present date:	£
(i) 14 Glenorchy Terrace, Edinburgh	100,000	(i) 10 Ventnor Terrace, Edinburgh	90,000
(ii) one-half interest in Scottish Widows Insurance Policy	6,449	(ii) one-half interest in Scottish Widows Insurance Policy	6,449
[(iii) 38.03% interest in C.C. Hornig & Son Ltd. Executive Pension Fund	54,390]	[(iii) 61.97% interest in C.C. Hornig & Son Ltd. Executive Fund	88,628]
[(iv) personal jewellery .	8,000]	[(iv) interest in Legal & General Pension Plan Policy	7,444]
		(v) interest in Liverpool and Victoria Insurance Policy	10,343
		(vi) shares in Abbey National	2,000
		(vii) cash in Bank of Scotland	3,567.22
		(viii) cash in Bank of Scotland	41,136.52
		(ix) shares in C.C. Hornig & Son Ltd	nil
		[(x) personal jewellery ..	8,000)]
SUBTOTAL	**106,449***	**SUBTOTAL**	**153,495.74***
Less		*Less*	
(a) mortgage	16,000	(a) mortgage	30,312
(b) one-half liability to Bank of Scotland	273.39	(b) one-half liability to Bank of Scotland	273.39
(c) cheque account overdraft with Bank of Scotland	2,000	(c) current account overdraft with Bank of Scotland	8,620
(d) legal fees	10,000	(d) legal fees	10,000
	28,273.39		49,205.39
TOTAL	**78,175.61**	**TOTAL**	**104,290.35**

*excludes (illiquid) pension(s) and personal jewellery

PART I OF DRAFT FAMILY LAW (SCOTLAND) BILL[1]

PARENTAL RESPONSIBILITIES AND RIGHTS, GUARDIANSHIP AND ADMINISTRATION OF CHILDREN'S PROPERTY

Parental responsibilities and rights

Parental responsibilities

1.—(1) A parent has in relation to his or her child the following responsibilities ("parental responsibilities"), that is to say, the responsibility—

(a) to safeguard and promote the child's health, development and welfare;

(b) to provide, in a manner appropriate to the stage of development of the child, direction and guidance to the child;

(c) if the child is not living with the parent, to maintain personal relations and direct contact with the child on a regular basis;

(d) to act as the child's legal representative,

but only in so far as compliance with paragraphs (a), (b), (c) or (d) above (as the case may be) is practicable and in the interests of the child.

(2) "Child" means for the purposes of—

(a) paragraphs (a) and (b) of subsection (1) above, a person under the age of 18 years;

(b) paragraphs (c) and (d) of that subsection, a person under the age of 16 years.

(3) Any reference in this Part of this Act to a person acting as the legal representative of a child is a reference to that person, in the interests of the child—

(a) administering any property belonging to the child; and

[1] Annexed to the Scottish Law Commission's *Report on Family Law* (Scot. Law Com. No. 135, 1992).

(b) acting in, or giving consent to, any transaction having legal effect where the child is incapable of so acting or consenting on his or her own behalf.

(4) This section is without prejudice to any duty imposed on a parent in relation to a child under any other enactment.

Parental rights

2.—(1) In order to enable a parent to fulfil his or her parental responsibilities, a parent shall have in relation to his or her child the following rights ("parental rights"), that is to say, the right—

(a) to have the child living with him or her or otherwise to regulate the child's residence;

(b) to control, direct or guide, in a manner appropriate to the stage of development of the child, the child's upbringing;

(c) if the child is not living with the parent, to maintain personal relations and direct contact with the child on a regular basis;

(d) to act as the child's legal representative.

(2) Where two or more persons have any parental right, each of them may exercise that right without the consent of the other person or, as the case may be, any of the other persons, unless any decree or deed conferring the right otherwise provides.

(3) Notwithstanding subsection (2) above, no person shall be entitled to remove a child from, or to retain a child outwith, the United Kingdom without the consent of a relevant person if the child was habitually resident in Scotland with that relevant person immediately before the removal or retention; and in this subsection "relevant person" means a parent or the parents of the child or any other person who has the right to control the child's residence.

(4) This section is without prejudice to any right conferred on a parent by any other provision of this Act or any other enactment.

(5) In this section "child" means a person under the age of 16 years.

Provisions relating to both parental responsibilities and rights

3.—(1) The parental responsibilities and parental rights of a parent shall not be dependent on that parent being or having been married to the other parent of the child concerned.

(2) Nothing in this Part of this Act shall affect any enactment or rule of law by virtue of which a person may be granted or deprived of parental responsibilities or parental rights.

(3) The fact that a person has parental responsibilities or parental rights in relation to a child shall not entitle that person to

act in any way which would be incompatible with any court decree relating to the child or the child's property, or any supervision requirement relating to the child made under section 44(1) of the Social Work (Scotland) Act 1968.

(4) A person who has parental responsibilities or parental rights in respect of a child may not surrender or transfer any part of those responsibilities or rights to another but may arrange for some or all of them to be met or exercised by one or more persons acting on his or her behalf.

(5) The person with whom any such arrangement is made may be a person who already has parental responsibilities or parental rights in respect of the child concerned.

(6) The making of any such arrangement shall not affect any liability of the person making it which may arise from any failure to meet any part of his or her parental responsibilities for the child concerned.

Protection of children from violence

4.—(1) In any proceedings (whether criminal or civil) against a person for striking a child, it shall not be a defence for the person to establish that he or she struck the child in the purported exercise of any parental right if he or she struck the child—
  (a) with a stick, belt or other object of whatever description; or
  (b) in such a way as to cause, or to risk causing—
      (i) injury; or
      (ii) pain or discomfort lasting more than a very short time.

(2) In section 12 of the Children and Young Persons (Scotland) Act 1937 the following are hereby repealed—
  (a) in subsection (1) the words "assaults," and "assaulted,";
  (b) subsection (7).

Persons without parental responsibilities or rights having care or control of child

5.—(1) A person over the age of 16 years who—
  (a) has care or control of a child under the age of 16 years; but
  (b) does not have parental responsibilities or parental rights in respect of that child, may do what is reasonable in all the circumstances of the case (and may in particular give consent to any medical or dental treatment or procedure where the child is not able to give such consent on his or her own behalf) for the purpose of safeguarding the child's health, development or welfare.

(2) Section 4 of this Act shall have effect in relation to a person

mentioned in subsection (1) above as if for the words "any parental right" there were substituted the words "a right of reasonable chastisement by virtue of having the care or control of the child".

(3) Nothing in this section shall apply to a person in so far as the person has care or control of a child in a school within the meaning of section 135(1) of the Education (Scotland) Act 1980.

Views of children

6.—(1) Before a person reaches a major decision which involves fulfilling a parental responsibility or exercising a parental right, the person shall, so far as practicable, ascertain the views of the child concerned regarding the decision, and shall give due consideration to those views, taking account of the child's age and maturity.

(2) Without prejudice to the generality of subsection (1) above, a child of the age of 12 years or more shall be presumed to have sufficient maturity to enable him or her to express a reasonable view regarding any such decision.

(3) A transaction entered into in good faith by a third party and a person acting as the legal representative of a child shall not be challengeable on the ground that the child was not consulted or that due consideration was not given to the child's views before the transaction was entered into.

Guardianship

Appointment of guardians

7.—(1) The parent of a child may appoint another individual to be guardian of the child after the parent's death, but any such appointment shall be of no effect unless —

(a) the appointment is in writing and signed by the parent; and

(b) the parent at the time of his or her death was entitled to act as the legal representative of the child or would have been so entitled if he or she had survived until after the birth of the child.

(2) A guardian of a child may appoint another individual to take his or her place as the child's guardian in the event of his or her death, but any such appointment shall be of no effect unless the appointment is in writing and signed by the person making the appointment.

(3) An appointment as guardian shall not take effect until

accepted, either expressly, or impliedly by acts which are not consistent with any other intention.

(4) If two or more persons are appointed as guardians, any one or more of them shall be entitled to accept office, even if both or all of them do not accept office, unless the appointment expressly provides otherwise.

(5) Subject to section 12 of this Act, a person appointed as a child's guardian under this section shall have in respect of the child the responsibilities imposed, and the rights conferred, on a parent by sections 1 and 2 of this Act respectively; and those sections and sections 3(2) to (6) of this Act shall apply in relation to a guardian as they apply in relation to a parent.

(6) A decision as to the appointment of a guardian under subsection (1) or (2) above shall be regarded for the purposes of section 6 of this Act or that section as applied by subsection (5) above as a major decision which involves exercising a parental right.

Revocation and other termination of appointment

8.—(1) An appointment under section 7(1) or (2) of this Act revokes an earlier such appointment (including one made in an unrevoked will or codicil) made by the same person in respect of the same child, unless it is clear (whether as a result of an express provision in the later appointment or by any necessary implication) that the purpose of the later appointment is to appoint an additional guardian.

(2) Subject to subsections (3) and (4) below, the revocation of an appointment under section 7(1) or (2) of this Act (including one made in an unrevoked will or codicil) shall not take effect unless the revocation is in writing and is signed by the person making the revocation.

(3) Any appointment under section 7(1) or (2) of this Act (other than one made in a will or codicil) is revoked if, with the intention of revoking the appointment, the person who made it—

    (a)   destroys the document by which it was made; or

    (b)   has some other person destroy that document in his presence.

(4) For the avoidance of doubt, an appointment under section 7(1) or (2) of this Act made in a will or codicil is revoked if the will or codicil is revoked.

(5) Once an appointment of a guardian has taken effect under section 7 of this Act, then, unless the terms of the appointment provide otherwise, it shall terminate only by virtue of—

    (a)   the child concerned attaining the age of 18 years;

(b) the death of the child or the guardian; or

(c) the termination of the appointment by a court order under section 12 of this Act.

Administration of child's property

Safeguarding of child's property

9.—(1) Subject to section 16 of this Act, this section applies where—

(a) property is owned by or due to a child;

(b) the property is held by a person other than a parent or guardian of the child; and

(c) but for this section, the property would be required to be transferred to a parent or guardian for administration by him or her on behalf of the child.

(2) Subject to subsection (4) below, where this section applies and the person holding the property is an executor or trustee, then—

(a) if the value of the property exceeds £20,000, the executor or trustee shall; or

(b) if that value is not less than £5000 and not more than £20,000, the executor or trustee may apply to the Accountant of Court for a direction as to the administration of the property.

(3) Subject to subsection (4) below, where this section applies and the person holding the property is a person other than an executor or trustee, then, if the value of the property is not less than £5000, that person may apply to the Accountant of Court for a direction as to the administration of the property.

(4) Where a parent or guardian of the child has been appointed a trustee under a trust deed to administer the property concerned, subsections (2) and (3) above shall not apply, and the executor, trustee or other person shall transfer the property to the parent or guardian.

(5) On receipt of an application under subsection (2) or (3) above, the Accountant of Court may—

(a) apply to the court for the appointment of a judicial factor to administer the property concerned, and in the event of the court appointing a judicial factor shall direct the property in relation to which the appointment has been made to be transferred to the factor;

(b) direct all or part of the property concerned to be

transferred to the Accountant of Court to be administered directly on behalf of the child; or

(c) direct all or part of the property to be transferred to a parent or guardian to be administered by him or her on behalf of the child.

(6) A direction under subsection (5)(c) above may include such conditions as the Accountant of Court considers appropriate, including in particular a condition—

(a) that in relation to that property no capital expenditure shall be incurred without the approval of the Accountant of Court; or

(b) that there shall be exhibited annually to the Accountant of Court the securities and bank books which represent the capital of the estate.

(7) A person who has applied under subsection (2) or (3) above for a direction shall not transfer the property concerned except in accordance with a direction under subsection (5) above.

(8) For the purposes of subsections (2) and (3) above, the Secretary of State may by regulations from time to time vary any sum referred to therein.

(9) The power to make regulations conferred by subsection (8) above shall be exercisable by statutory instrument which shall be subject to annulment in pursuance of a resolution of either House of Parliament.

(10) In this section "child" means a person under the age of 16 years who is habitually resident in Scotland.

Obligations and rights of person administering child's property

10.—(1) A person, on ceasing to act as a child's legal representative, shall be liable to account to the child for his or her intromissions with the child's property.

(2) A person shall not be liable to the child in respect of any of the child's funds which have been used in the proper discharge of the person's responsibility to safeguard and promote the child's health, development or welfare.

(3) A person acting as a child's legal representative in relation to the administration of the child's property—

(a) shall be required to act as a reasonable and prudent person would act on his or her own behalf; and

(b) subject to section 12 of this Act, shall be entitled to do anything in relation to it that the child could do if of full age and capacity.

Court Orders

Application for court order

11.—(1) Any person claiming an interest may make an application under this section to the court for an order relating to—

(a) parental responsibilities;

(b) parental rights;

(c) guardianship; or

(d) the administration of a child's property.

(2) Any application under this section may be made in a consistorial action or in proceedings in the Court of Session or sheriff court which are independent of a consistorial action.

(3) An application may be made under this section by the child concerned.

(4) It shall be incompetent for a local authority to make an application under this section except for such an order as is referred to in section 12(1)(c) or (d) of this Act.

(5) Any reference in this section and in sections 12 and 13 of this Act to an order includes a reference to an interim order or to an order varying or discharging an order.

Disposal of application under s.11

12.—(1) On an application being made to it under section 11 of this Act, the court may make such order relating to the matters mentioned in subsection (1) of that section as it thinks fit and may in particular make any of the following orders—

(a) an order ("a residence order") regulating the arrangements to be made as to the person with whom a child under the age of 16 years is to live;

(b) an order ("a contact order") regulating the arrangements to be made for maintaining personal relations and direct contact between a child under the age of 16 years and a parent, or other person, with whom the child is not, or will not be, living;

(c) an order ("a specific issue order") regulating any specific question which has arisen, or which may arise, in connection with any of the matters mentioned in section 11(1) of this Act;

(d) an interdict prohibiting the taking of any step, which is of a kind specified in the interdict, in the exercise of parental responsibilities or parental rights or rights of guardianship relating to a child or in the administration of a child's property;

(e)   an order appointing a judicial factor to manage a child's property or remitting the matter to the Accountant of Court to report on suitable arrangements for the future management of the property.

(2) The court may make an order under this section in a consistorial action—

(a)   whether or not an application has been made for such an order under section 11 of this Act; or

(b)   even if the court refuses to grant the principal remedy sought in the action.

(3) In any proceedings under this section, the court shall regard the welfare of the child concerned as the paramount consideration and shall not make any order under this section unless it is satisfied that to do so will be in the interests of the child and, in particular, that making the order will be better for the child than making no such order at all:

Provided that nothing in this subsection shall adversely affect the position of a person who has acquired any property of a child, or any right or interest in such property, in good faith and for value.

(4) The court may in an order under this section—

(a)   deprive a person of some or all of his or her parental responsibilities or parental rights,

(b)   appoint or remove a guardian.

(5) In considering whether to make an order under this section the court shall give due consideration to the ascertainable views of the child concerned which are properly before the court, taking account of the child's age and maturity; and, without prejudice to the foregoing provisions of this subsection, a child of the age of 12 years or more shall be presumed to have sufficient maturity to enable him or her to express a reasonable view.

(6) Nothing in subsection (5) above shall require a child to be legally represented if the child is not a party to the proceedings.

Effect of court orders under s.12

13.—(1) An order under section 12 of this Act by which a person acquires a parental responsibility or parental right shall deprive any other person of a parental responsibility or parental right only in so far as the order expressly so provides and only to the extent necessary to give effect to the order.

(2) Where the court makes a residence order to the effect that a child is to live with a person who is not the child's parent or guardian, that person shall have parental responsibilities and

parental rights in respect of the child while the residence order remains in force.

Restrictions on decrees for divorce or annulment affecting children

14.—(1) In any action for divorce or for a declarator of nullity of marriage, the court shall consider—

(a)   whether there are any children of the family to whom this section applies; and

(b)   where there are any such children, whether (in the light of information before the court as to the arrangements which have been, or are proposed to be, made for their upbringing) it should exercise the powers conferred on it by section 12 of this Act, or section 37(1B) of the Social Work (Scotland) Act 1968, with respect to any of them.

(2) Where, in any case to which this section applies, it appears to the court that—

(a)   the circumstances of the case require it, or are likely to require it, to exercise any of its powers under section 12 of this Act, or the said section 37(1B), with respect to any such child;

(b)   it is not in a position to exercise such a power without giving further consideration to the case; and

(c)   there are exceptional circumstances which make it desirable in the interests of the child that it should not grant decree in the action until it is in a position to exercise such a power,

it shall postpone its decision on the granting of decree in the action until it is in such a position.

(3) This section applies to any child of the family who has not reached the age of 16 years at the date when the court considers the case in accordance with the requirements of this section.

(4) In this section "child of the family", in relation to the parties to a marriage, means—

(a)   a child of both of those parties; and

(b)   any other child, not being a child who is placed with those parties as foster parents by a local authority or voluntary organisation, who has been treated by both of those parties as a child of their family.

Treatment in consistorial actions etc of children requiring compulsory measures of care

15.—In section 37 of the Social Work (Scotland) Act 1968 after subsection (1A) there shall be inserted the following subsections—

"(1B) Where it appears to the court in the course of any proceedings to which this subsection applies that a child is in need of compulsory measures of care by reason that any of the conditions mentioned in paragraphs (a) to (f) and (gg) of section 32(2) of this Act is satisfied with respect to the child, it may refer the matter to the reporter specifying the relevant condition.

(1C) subsection (1B) above applies to—
  (a)   an action for divorce or for a declarator of marriage, nullity of marriage, parentage or non-parentage;
  (b)   proceedings relating to parental responsibilities or parental rights or rights of guardianship within the meaning of Part I of the Family Law (Scotland) Act 1992;
  (c)   proceedings for an adoption order under the Adoption (Scotland) Act 1978 or for an order under section 18 of that Act declaring a child free for adoption.".

Awards of damages to children

16.—(1) Where in any court proceedings a sum of money becomes payable to, or for the benefit of, a person under legal disability by reason of non-age, the court may make such order relating to the payment and management of that sum for the benefit of that person as it thinks fit.

(2) Without prejudice to the generality of subsection (1) above, the court may in an order under this section—
  (a)   appoint a judicial factor to invest, apply or otherwise deal with the money for the benefit of the person concerned;
  (b)   order the money to be paid to the sheriff clerk or the Accountant of Court, to be invested, applied or otherwise dealt with, under the directions of the court, for the benefit of that person;
  (c)   order the money to be paid to a parent or guardian of that person, to be invested, applied or otherwise dealt with, under the directions of the court, for the benefit of that person; or
  (d)   order the money to be paid directly to that person.

(3) The receipt of any person to whom payment is made in accordance with an order under this section shall be a sufficient discharge of the obligation to make the payment.

Choice of law rules and jurisdiction

Parental responsibilities and parental rights and guardianship
   17.—(1) Subject to subsection (2) below, any question arising as to parental responsibilities or parental rights, or as to the responsibilities or rights of a guardian, in relation to a child shall be determined by the law of the place of the child's habitual residence at the time when the question arises.
   (2) Any question concerning the immediate protection of a child shall be determined by the law of the place where the child is when the question arises.
   (3) The foregoing provisions of this section are without prejudice to section 12(3) of this Act.
   (4) Any question arising as to whether a person is validly appointed or constituted as guardian of a child shall be determined by the law of the place of the child's habitual residence on the date when the appointment was made or the event constituting the guardianship occurred.
   (5) For the purposes of subsection (4) above, if the appointment was made by will, the date of the appointment shall be regarded as the date of death of the testator.

Jurisdiction in relation to administration of child's property
   18.—(1) The Court of Session shall have jurisdiction to entertain an application for an order relating to the administration of a child's property if the child is habitually resident, or the property is situated, in Scotland.
   (2) A sheriff shall have jurisdiction to entertain such an application if the child is habitually resident, or the property is situated, in the sheriffdom.

Interpretation of Part I
   19.—In this Part of this Act—
   "consistorial action" means an action for divorce or for a declarator of marriage, nullity of marriage, parentage or non-parentage;
   "parental responsibilities" has the meaning assigned by section 1 of this Act;
   "parental rights" has the meaning assigned by section 2 of this Act;
   "transaction" has the same meaning as in section 9 of the Age of Legal Capacity (Scotland) Act 1991.

Index